Torn by Light

Books by Joanne de Longchamps

And Ever Venus (1944)
Eden Under Glass (1957)
The Hungry Lions (1963)
The Wishing Animal (1970)
The Schoolhouse Poems (1975)
One Creature: Poems & Collages (1977)
Warm-Bloods, Cold-Bloods: Poems & Collages (1981)
Torn by Light: Selected Poems (1993)

Western Literature Series

Torn
by Light

Selected Poems
Joanne de Longchamps

Edited by Shaun T. Griffin

Foreword by Harold Witt

University of Nevada Press   *Reno   Las Vegas   London*

Western Literature Series Editor: John H. Irsfeld

A list of books in the series follows the index.

The paper used in this book meets the requirements of American National Standard for Information Sciences— Permanence of Paper for Printed Library Materials, ANSI Z39.48–1984. Binding materials were selected for strength and durability.

Library of Congress Cataloging-in-Publication Data
De Longchamps, Joanne
    Torn by light : selected poems / Joanne de Longchamps ;
    edited by Shaun T. Griffin ; foreword by Harold Witt.
    Shaun T. Griffin ; foreword by Harold Witt.
        p.   cm. — (Western literature series)
    Includes index.
    ISBN 0-87417-218-7 (cloth) — ISBN 0-87417-217-9
(paper)
    I. Griffin, Shaun T. (Shaun Timothy), 1953–   . II. Title.
III. Series.
    PS3507.E527A6   1993
    811'.54–dc20   92-40531
                                                               CIP

Frontispiece: Joanne de Longchamps, ca. 1982 (photo by Ted Cook). Cover art: *Dragonfly,* from *One Creature: Poems & Collages,* by Joanne de Longchamps. Courtesy of Thomas Wright (photo by Peter Walker). Jacket stamping adapted from *Dragonfly.*

University of Nevada Press, Reno, Nevada 89557 USA
Copyright © 1993 University of Nevada Press
All rights reserved
Design by Milenda Nan Ok Lee
Printed in the United States of America
9 8 7 6 5 4 3 2 1

"And what is it about Greece that makes you like it
so much?" asked some one.
I smiled. "The light and the poverty," I said.
"You're a romantic," said the man.
"Yes," I said, "I'm crazy enough to believe that the
happiest man on earth is the man with the fewest
needs. And I also believe that if you have light,
such as you have here, all ugliness is obliterated.
Since I've come to your country I know light is holy:
Greece is a holy land to me."

Henry Miller
The Colossus of Maroussi

"There is a quality of air and light and movement of
light and shadow that I saw in the Aegean that is
(at) Pyramid Lake."

Joanne de Longchamps
Interview, 1980

Contents

The Hungry Lions, 1963

The Wishing Animal, 1970

One Creature: Poems & Collages, 1977

Warm-Bloods, Cold-Bloods: Poems & Collages, 1981

The Glass Hammer (posthumous manuscript), 1983

Illustrations

Foreword

Joanne de Longchamps is the quintessential poet. She was one uninvolved in the self-promotion that has become de rigueur even among the arts. Thoroughly modern, both in viewpoint and execution, she practiced her art like the great poets of the past, true to an inner ideal rather than writing for more obvious rewards. In an era of the "Big Sell" it's difficult to tell who's who and what's what. We can only test poetry on our pulses to see if it's real or not.

And if we test Joanne de Longchamps's poetry in this way we discover it to be, contained as it is in its forms, living and breathing, and speaking to us. After the early influence of Edna St. Vincent Millay that was exemplified in Joanne's first book, *And Ever Venus* (1944), she less and less often wrote sonnets or fixed forms. But that discipline is present, and as her lines become freer they still have an echoing music, subtle rhyme, and power of imagery that is lacking in much contemporary verse. The Beat influence no longer has the power it once had, and poets are now beginning to rediscover what Joanne knew all along: poetry is a craft and not only a freedom.

In her second book, *Eden Under Glass* (1957), there is a definite loosening of strictures and a widening of subject matter. A young woman's responses to love and nature no longer predominate. And though she continues to dramatize herself as the central figure in many of the poems, she is also a citizen—as in "Jury

Duty"—and not sure justice is being done: "A verdict is one other word to hear." Lines like this place her among the poets we remember.

She shows us in "The Young Men Dream of Women" an image only an artist's eye is capable of seeing: Godiva is "sheathed in her swaying hair / that falls like mountain water on pale flanks / of mare and rider." When she wrote those lines, she was already an artist in the media of paint and brush, and pen and ink. She was about to begin her unique career as a collagist, which would be reflected in the last two books published before her death: *One Creature* and *Warm-Bloods, Cold-Bloods*, where collage complemented poem. In the latter, we are treated to a picture of Godiva in marvelous paper art as well as in the poem. Felicitous phrases abound—"the whitest silence," "thin towers of conversation," "rapier rains"—setting this poet's work apart from those who merely try.

A cat lover, she took lions as her symbol, and in the The Hungry Lions (1963) several lion poems make the book thematic. Some of the images—"rayed manes ringleted," "Swiftly are warm hands / surprised into a shape of paws"—were included in her lion collage, later published with the title poem ("The Hungry Lions") in *One Creature*, an ecological idea (that all of us are one) more and more pertinent to the saving of the planet. *The Hungry Lions* ends with the remarkable "A Mathematic of Change," an externalizing of the traumatic experience of mastectomy. This was one of the many tribulations of Joanne de Longchamps's life, which strengthened her poetry and opened her later work to subjects she would have considered unpoetic in earlier years. *The Hungry Lions* is also notable for three poems of reminiscence, which are among my personal favorites: "Reunion," "Echoes from the Playground," and the moving image of her father, "Ask Why I Dream." In these there are no lions, no gods, but a clear looking backward to when she was "sorceress of sticks and stones," when a family got together at Christmas time in a "tall house flanked by gum trees / and a remnant orchard brittle in December," and when her father was "the dandy of [her] childhood / rocking in his broken shoes." Such precisions of memory are another facet of this remarkable poet, and perhaps equal Roethke's childhood scenes, or Dylan Thomas's, and take off the top of our heads, as Emily Dickinson said was her way of knowing a poem.

An abiding interest in Greece and things Grecian enlarges the scope of *The Wishing Animal* (1970), which also further reveals her preoccupation with beasts, masks, stones, and crystals. A trip to the cradle of democracy deeply influenced her fourth collection of poetry and her collages. The animal theme is evident in *One Creature* and in the second part of *Warm-Bloods, Cold-Bloods*; the Grecian theme appears in the third part. "Go gold, outdazzle fate," Joanne exhorts us, and herself, in "A Defense of Masks," and she praises pretense—a key to some of the poems. Always she believed life could be an art. Man is "the wishing animal," which sets him apart from the beasts. Joanne wished Greece, and went; she wished poetry and art, and made them; she wished life, and had it over and over. In "Coming to Life," she "made a tempting bed for death," but "that goat of love" ate the wreathes and toppled the urns. She decided to stay a while longer in spite of tragedies, the worst, a son's suicide, yet to come.

What often saved her was humor, the sense of which she had in abundance, though this is not always evident in the poems. The comic turns of phrase of "A Bedlam Story" show yet another facet of Joanne de Longchamps that places her beyond what most of her contemporaries could do. Amid some of the more somber philosophizing of *The Wishing Animal*, we find "her widow's tics and talks;" "just pretend to listen and let her ventilate;" and "He thought she was an ancient fan / wheeling on his ceiling."

The Schoolhouse Poems (1975), many of them written at the old renovated schoolhouse at Galena Creek where she spent much of her time for some years, repoems in her earlier books. Some of the poems in this collection have a refreshing directness, the thing itself as symbol, and responses to dailiness. Her memorable "Diary Entry: Galena Creek," with the unforgettable image of lizards as "dragons doing pushups," is equaled, however, by the close observation of the African landscape in "Four from Africa," four poems that resulted from a journey there. In the final section, "on the edge," she can be, when not going in gold and masked, remarkably candid about her despair: in "Sub—*prefix. 1. Under, beneath, below; as in*" she is "found / crouched in the broom-closet; drunk, raging, weeping." She teaches us bravery in the face of dire, death-threatening cancer. She can even be humorous about such things. About radiation she says, "I am a six-minute egg / cooked daily for six weeks," and "I've made a game / to play against lopsided moons." In "Letter to the Editor" she laughs raucously at an editor of *Harper's Bazaar*, who had advised "Be proud of your body. Revel in it." "I have 31 surgical scars . . ." she responds, and "To hell with *Harper's Bazaar*."

In her last years, collage art and poetry were almost equally important to her, the one illuminating and enhancing the other. This interest culminated in two previously mentioned volumes of collage and poems from *West Coast Poetry Review*, which are unique among poetry books. Most of the poems in *One Creature*, some accompanied by collage, are from previous collections—a gathering together of the animal poems she was so deft at making. *Warm-Bloods, Cold-Bloods* has the dual theme of the human and the nonhuman animal. It is introduced by the poem to her son, "Letters to Dare," from whose tragic suicide she never recovered, although the poem seems to overcome the grief. She wrote those words about his suicide, she created the cloud-country collages, and the Snow-Queen with its glowing-eyed wolf. I have not read another poem so deeply moving about the mother-son relationship.

Joanne de Longchamps's belief in the healing power of poetry never wavered. Before her death she was putting together another collection, *The Glass Hammer*. Some of those poems are incorporated in this book. She lived in a world of art which could not, finally, save her, except as she is saved here, alive in words and collage. And here she is resurrected, to be seen in a different light of time. The poems retain the power they had when they were written. This collection will show her as among the best of her contemporaries: original, marvelous, magical.

Harold Witt
Orinda, California
March 1991

Preface

From those first timid strokes of the pen in *And Ever Venus*—twenty modest poems, mostly sonnets on love and nature—to the last desperate cries in *The Glass Hammer*, Joanne de Longchamps gave us poetry and collage through the eyes of a woman, a visionary of her time. Having read her later works for years, I was struck with the simplicity, the very careful borders within which her first chapbook was undertaken. These poems seemed shards of what was to come. Bashful, reticent, still wary of free verse, she spoke in rhymed stanzas, not knowing how far she would travel with her art: "I know it [my heart] to be candid, without art." We can only wonder if she meant "without guile." The chapbook was part of the poetry series Destiny Editions, edited by Dion O'Donnol.

With *Eden Under Glass*, de Longchamps took the first steps toward a fuller, richer poetry, started to let her hair down and write poems on new themes. Whether it was through early feminism, or anti-atomic sentiment, she shook the reader with her observations. Two in particular document life in the fifties: "Tea-Time: Atomic Age," a sober portrait of the housewife "ringed with . . . dry mist of cigarettes"; and "Exitus," a revealing look at Oppenheimer—"World there was / that spun in darkness down." Both poems were written long before objection to nuclear war became fashionable.

In this second book, one can see her early fascination

with mythology—which later became a strong personal mythology as well—and how she wove it into her poems, collages, and thinking, so that it finally drove her to write through the spell of Greek myth. She was as conversant in the Greek roots of words as is a chef with spice. Still most comfortable in the sonnet form, she took more chances and the range of her subjects grew in *Eden Under Glass*. These poems were a natural development for her: she wanted more from them and learned she could take more liberties with language.

The Hungry Lions was the next major literary step for de Longchamps. When one looks in the back of the book and finds her predecessors in the Indiana University Press Poetry Series to be Carolyn Kizer, David Wagoner, Conrad Aiken, Josephine Miles, Theodore Roethke, and García Lorca in translation, it's easy to understand what a phenomenal leap this was for her. Hers was the twenty-fifth book published in the series. It was 1963, the year Kennedy would be shot down. She was still relatively young—forty years old—and to have landed among the literary company in that list was no small feat. It saddens one to think she would not end her life as so many of the others in that series, a well-known poet. She was a Nevadan, and that came to define her existence as being separate and apart from mainstream literary America.

Her next book, *The Wishing Animal*, published by Vanderbilt University Press, was by far her most substantive, authoritative, and challenging book of poetry to date. With the publication of that volume, her work clearly moved into a new voice—dramatic, delicate, and precise: "Our blood / enters the earth, / black wine / for the thirsty stones." These are poems that writhe on the page—that move in and out of the reader with ease and still manage to mystify, to terrify, and to restore. Many of these poems informed her collages—later collected in limited-edition, small-press volumes—and she began to define herself as much a collage artist as poet.

Then came what some of her peers think is her strongest collection of poetry, *The Schoolhouse Poems*, from a Nevada publisher, William Fox. This volume marks her days spent on a family acre near Galena Creek, the site of a one-room schoolhouse. The title page is Robert Caples's eerie portrait of de Longchamps, painted in 1975. Once again she returns to nature (this time in Nevada), travel, and a fellow writer in "Late Letter to Walter Clark." She remembers friends gathered on a "snowhill / for the opening and closing / of cold earth given you," and finds a way to say good-bye using his words in her poem: " 'a hawk sailed up / out of the white mountain,' " a most respectful tribute to her friend and fellow author. Many writers and painters influenced de Longchamps throughout her life; Walter Clark was among her closest of friends. Even in the late 1960s he was critiquing her prose, encouraging her to write more of it. His quote on the book jacket of *The Wishing Animal* began "Joanne de Longchamps is a true poet."

Though de Longchamps spent a lifetime observing and recreating Nevada's acute light, air, and soil, it wasn't until *The Schoolhouse Poems* that she really began to write about Nevada the *place*. Perhaps this was due to her early belief in Greece, in animals, and finally in the power of art to transform these two into a personal mythology that would sustain her until the landscape of the Great Basin became part of that myth. Certainly her interest in the physical environment was heightened by living at the tree-line, under the watchful eye of hawk, squirrel, and owl.

William L. Fox would remain her publisher for the rest of her life. Were it not for the fine work of West Coast Poetry Review, her collages would not be preserved today. The collages focus on the themes that drove her poetry: mythology, animals, death, and the cross between science and poetry. Though many of the collages were wonderful recreations of the human body, none depicted her personal struggle with failing health. The majority of the poems in *One Creature* were taken from earlier collections, but seen here with the collages they dazzle the reader in red, blue, and all hues in between. She was unrelenting in her search for the right words: "tracery, hymenopteron, sievings." *One Creature* is scientifically precise—the poetry captures the essence of life forms: "Yet bees dance. / Their pre-prescribed circling, / set to sun's position, / reveals (to bees) / the direction of suitable pollen."

In these poems she strives to capture the color, sound, and motion of survival, and links them to our own struggle, our own inexplicable journey. In her poem "Cygnus," she likens marriage to the swan's monogamous mating: "We choose as swan or skylark. It is said / the swan sings only as it dies."

De Longchamps likened us to mammalian, plant,

and mythological life, drawing parallel connections between the animal and human. In these parallels she saw larger ones—the ghost of the sea bear—and smaller ones too, in the geometry of the beehive. But precision, a desire to know and represent the thing in its fullest, is the miracle of these poems and collages.

She continues this story with *Warm-Bloods, Cold-Bloods.* Her eel, jellyfish, and bat poem-collages have made Nevada schoolchildren from Dyer to Battle Mountain shudder. They cannot believe one woman made such striking pictures from scrap paper *after* she wrote a poem about that very creature. This is art at its finest: from child to adult, she speaks our language, tells our story, and makes us quiver with recognition.

Her tragic and elegiac poem to her son Dare is surely one of the finest to have been written from a mother to a son in this century. None but stone could read it and be unmoved. Friends say she never got over his loss. It is a miracle she could go on at all, with the medical complications in her own life.

In her last collection, the posthumous manuscript *The Glass Hammer*, de Longchamps chronicles the rituals of a failed body, struggle with drink, and killing pain. The only time I spoke to her was during this last, horribly painful period in her life. I called to ask if she would read in a group of very well known poets—Carolyn Kizer, Mark Strand, William Matthews, Richard Shelton, and Pamela Stewart—who were coming to Reno to read in the Piñon Poetry Series. She declined in a raspy voice, but was "so honored" that I asked her. She did not feel she could do justice to the reading, her health getting worse by the day. I pleaded with her to reconsider but knew it was futile. And when I hung up I knew also that I had been in the presence of something much larger than I—a woman of conviction, of humility, of genuine beauty.

Throughout de Longchamps's life there was an absence of religious belief; her belief was in Greece, animals, and, ultimately, in the struggle between love and death: "We're afraid of being without love. And we're afraid of death." Nowhere was this struggle more acutely expressed than in love. She could *breathe* love—"My love, I know no more of love to say"—and be merciless too—"Not in a firm-fleshed beginning / are love's disguises known." This opening line is from "Grimdeath and the Bones": "Lovers die but caution kills / the living while they move." From her earliest work—"I love—in loving I was never wise"—to her last—"It is love, the artisan, the glassblower / . . . who takes our fragments into flame"—she wed the emotion to words until finally it became "a vessel / holding light once more."

Over the years, some readers have objected to de Longchamps's frequent use of alliteration in her poems, as in these lines from "Sea Bear": "He hears / the shaping sound the sea shakes / scooping sills and raising lintels." Clearly there is a fine line between language choice for specific accent and imitation of subject and overuse. This is an example of overuse; however, alliteration was one part of a voice de Longchamps strove to develop which, on the whole, strengthened the music within the lines of her poetry: "His death / is sharp, a shape of skill." (All poems in this book retain the author's original spelling, punctuation, and grammar in order to preserve her original intent.)

Reading de Longchamps's poems, it is interesting to note the poets who influenced her over the years—from Frost to Williams, Yeats, Wilbur, Kumin, and others—when in fact her writing often resembled the fine work of Plath, Sexton, and Vassar Miller. Many of her poems start with that Milleresque voice—the membrane thinned with pain or human frailty that both were subjected to. It was sheer strength that kept de Longchamps alive: "Survival is knowing what to lose— / then letting go."

Toward the end of her life de Longchamps was asked if living in Nevada had in some way limited her career as an artist. To this she responded "If I had wanted to be great I suppose I'd have gone to New York or I'd have gone back to Hollywood and picked up my contacts. What I want is the feeling of being around people who sense and try to create or recreate this marvel of just being alive. . . . I don't believe in all of this, the rewards of position and power. . . . No, I don't think Nevada is a cop-out at all." Nevertheless, there is little doubt that in her case, the very thing that she loved—the desert—kept her from a wider audience. How ironic that she should create in a sparse and elemental land, yet know this would exclude her from serious artistic recognition.

If this editor has any reward for his work, it must be the *act of reading* itself. With de Longchamps, I love reading her work, am stunned by its natural musical

quality and its stubborn insistence on precise nomen-
clature. In a poem from *One Creature*, she finds three
words whose definition is reddish brown: chestnut,
sorrel, and bay. Later, in the same poem is a similar
word play (brindle, dapple, fleck) to connote spots on
an animal. How can she describe such color and shape
in nature with unbridled ease? She remains a mystery,
her art having championed science with the most un-
likely heroes: the bee, dragonfly, salamander, seal, and
polar bear. A poetry exact. Just as she survived, so do
her words—unflinching yet humane. She gave us art
in collage and word, and in doing so gave everything
she had.

Shaun T. Griffin
Virginia City, Nevada
March–July 1992

Acknowledgments

This volume could not have been completed without
the tireless assistance of Joanne's friends, colleagues,
family, and others who, in the words of Ahmed Essa,
"feared that Joanne would be forgotten." Thus they
worked doubly hard to make the job of editing that
much easier. My thanks to the many people who shared
time, memories, letters, photographs, interviews, col-
lages, and more on behalf of the legacy of Joanne de
Longchamps: Jim McCormick, professor of art emeri-
tus, University of Nevada, Reno—without whom
this project simply could not have been completed;
Robert E. Blesse, Special Collections Library, Univer-

sity of Nevada, Reno; Roseanne Olds, volunteer, Black Rock Press, University of Nevada, Reno; William L. Fox, executive director, Nevada State Council on the Arts; Thomas Radko, director, University of Nevada Press—who encouraged me from the beginning to work on this project; Harold Witt, poet and Joanne's lifelong friend and confidant; Patricia Klos, librarian, McQueen High School; A. Wilber Stevens and James Hazen, professors, English department, University of Nevada, Las Vegas; Patricia Tissier-Martin, friend of Joanne's; Ahmed Essa, professor of English emeritus, University of Nevada, Reno; Barbara Agonia—whose original research on Joanne's poetry broke ground for this book; Pauline Nichols, who cared for Joanne in her final years; Joan Arrizabalaga and Patty Atcheson, dear friends of Joanne's; Barbara Rice, Joanne's first cousin, who helped track down endless leads and facts; Robert and Joyce Laxalt for sharing their memories; Grace Bordewich, long-time friend of Galen and Joanne; Barbara Hall, former director, Piñon Gallery; Beverlee Shafer and Audrey Sheppard, close friends; Kathleen Breeden—who painstakingly transcribed Joanne's last interview on tape; Donathan L. Bush, writer, Virginia City, for listening, reading, and caring; and many others who shared willingly their knowledge of Joanne to complete a sketch of what can only be seen as a beautiful, if tragic, life.

Every attempt was made to locate Galen DeLongchamps, but to no avail. The editor regrets that he was not able to talk with Mr. DeLongchamps prior to this book's publication.

Thank you to the hundreds of Nevada students who

led me to believe that Joanne's poetry and collages could make such an impact on young and old alike.

Finally, I would like to dedicate this book to the poets who came before us to cross Nevada's red sea; and to my parents, Daniel and Jean; and family—Deborah, Nevada, and Cody—you give me light, no matter how grave the dark.

Shaun T. Griffin

Permissions

Grateful acknowledgment is hereby made for the following permissions:

To William L. Fox, executor for the literary estate of Joanne de Longchamps, for permission to reprint selections from: *And Ever Venus* (Copyright 1944 Wagon and Star Publishers; Los Angeles, California); *The Schoolhouse Poems* (Copyright 1975 West Coast Poetry Review; Reno, Nevada); *One Creature* (Copyright 1977 West Coast Poetry Review; Reno, Nevada); *Warm-Bloods, Cold-Bloods* (Copyright 1981 West Coast Poetry Review; Reno, Nevada); *The Glass Hammer* (unpublished manuscript, 1983).

To Golden Quill Press for permission to reprint selections from *Eden Under Glass* (Copyright 1957 The Golden Quill Press; Francestown, New Hampshire).

To Indiana University Press for permission to reprint selections from *The Hungry Lions* (Copyright 1963 Indiana University Press; Bloomington, Indiana).

To Vanderbilt University Press for permission to reprint selections from *The Wishing Animal* (Copyright

Biography
Joanne de Longchamps (1923—1983)

She was born Joanne (Joan) Laurie Cutten in Los Angeles on January 7, 1923, "a true Capricorn," the daughter of Ruth Avery (Cutten) and Alfred Beverly "Bev" Cutten. Her father was a building contractor in Hollywood, but after the depression it was extremely difficult for him to make a living in the building trade. Ruth Avery was a dancer and performer on the vaudeville Orpheum circuit from 1919 to 1920, and encouraged her daughter to pursue the arts and drama at an early age (de Longchamps would later recall writing her first poem at age five). After her parents divorced when she was ten, Joan Cutten and her mother moved in with Ruth's mother, Minnie Buck (a widow) in the Hollywood Hills. De Longchamps was eleven: "I was an only child and my mother was my world."

As a young girl, cats, dolls, books, and poetry were her "unceasing joy."

When she was twelve, she and her mother sailed to England where she modeled (Patty Atcheson's watercolor portrait of de Longchamps is from a photograph of her during this period), and then moved on to France, where she took private art lessons from the British landscape painter Agnes Goodsir (teaching in Paris at the time). Six particularly long months were spent in a boarding school, the Institut de Saint Pierre in Paris, where she studied painting, music, and French. After a year abroad, she and her mother returned to Los Angeles, where de Longchamps enrolled in Fairfax

High School. There she acted in and designed costumes for the play "Swing It, Mother Goose," which her mother produced in 1937. Six of her poems were published in the Fairfax High Creative Writing Yearbook in 1938. In 1939, de Longchamps's first play was produced in Los Angeles, "With Blueberry Sauce." She completed her last two years of high school at the Chouinard Art Institute, where she studied watercolor and still-life painting. After high school de Longchamps studied at Los Angeles City College for a year and a half, where she was a contributor to the student humor magazine *Point*.

At seventeen, on a summer vacation in Reno, she met the man who "unfolded himself and he kept unfolding forever," Galen Edward DeLongchamps, the adopted son of the noted Nevada architect, Fredric Joseph DeLongchamps (he designed several neoclassical buildings in downtown Reno—the post office and the courthouse, for example—and other buildings in Carson City). Ruth Cutten pleaded with her daughter not to marry until she was eighteen, and de Longchamps relented. The ceremony was held in Pasadena, California, in 1941 ("I thought, Jesus I've got to have this"). When she and her groom left Los Angeles for Reno—young Galen's home—she changed the spelling of her first name from Joan to Joanne, and her new last name from DeLongchamps to de Longchamps, reflecting a more European spelling. There they would settle in an English cottage at 4 Elm Court, built by Fredric DeLongchamps circa 1929, possibly as his honeymoon cottage.

With the outbreak of World War II, de Longchamps

and Reno poet Irene Bruce took over the editing of the literary magazine *Destinies*, which was published at Lake Tahoe. The previous editor, Dion O'Donnol (also de Longchamps's first publisher), was drafted into service. It was through this little magazine that she met Harold Witt, a conscientious objector living at a C.O. camp at nearby Galena Creek. He sent *Destinies* some poems, and the two editors invited him to join the Reno Poetry Workshop. De Longchamps, Harold Witt, Irene Bruce, and Thelma "Brownie" Ireland formed the nucleus of a thriving literary community in Reno. De Longchamps would continue to correspond with her good friend and fellow poet Harold Witt for a lifetime.

A long-time student at the University of Nevada, Reno, de Longchamps never completed her degree because of a "history requirement," but over the next twenty years she audited literally every class the art department offered—ceramics, collage, painting— and many others, doing all the work required, though receiving no grade. In the 1940s she took watercolor and still-life classes from Helen Joslin, one of the few art instructors in the department at the time, though de Longchamps recalls that she "never felt like . . . an artist."

On October 7, 1949, Galen and Joanne de Longchamps had their only child, Galen Dare de Longchamps. For most of his career, the elder Galen worked as a mining engineer and a public schoolteacher.

In the 1950s and 1960s Robert Hartman, Craig Sheppard, and Edward Yates (de Longchamps would have an exhibition with Yates in 1967) influenced her artistic development. It was Robert Hartman who suggested she work in the collage medium (myriad scraps of paper torn and arranged precisely on paper to create an image). There were other artists in the community who had an impact on de Longchamps, and she on them: Robert Cole Caples (his portrait of her was printed on the cover page of *The Schoolhouse Poems*), Richard Guy Walton, and Zoray Andrus. During this time de Longchamps frequently collaborated with Elizabeth "Betty" Bliss, a painter and dear friend (several poems are dedicated to her, "Hospital Visit" for one). Also of importance at the university was her association with English professors Robert Hume, Charlton Laird, and Ahmed Essa. At Robert Hume's retirement in 1975, she wrote a beautiful unpublished poem dedicated to him.

On January 8, 1956, de Longchamps had an exhibition of twenty paintings and gave a lecture on poetry in the old Nevada Art Gallery at 643 Ralston Street in Reno.

De Longchamps's father, "Bev" Cutten, passed away in the 1950s. Though she had little contact with him as an adult, many of her poems recall his influence ("Ask Why I Dream").

Joanne, Galen, and Dare made two trips to Greece on tours sponsored by *Greek Heritage* magazine in 1965 and 1971. On their second journey to Greece they continued on to Africa, where she kept copious notes, which were later used in her poems and collages. She revered what those ethereal places held for her: myth, consequence, definition.

According to Jim McCormick, professor of art emeritus, when de Longchamps returned "it animated her work for years." She later recalled working on a collage "on her dining room table and Betty Bliss was mumbling to herself about Zeus and all of these things." De Longchamps and Bliss referred to themselves as "the Greekniks."

De Longchamps held two collage exhibitions in 1967. The "Toward Greece Series" was at the University Gallery in the Church Fine Arts building on the University of Nevada, Reno, campus from March 6 to 29. The "Toward Greece Series" was later published in the literary magazine *Trace* (1968). The Las Vegas Art League sponsored the second show in Las Vegas from August 20 to September 15. Several of these collages were inspired by Ovid's *Metamorphoses*, and others by Rimbaud's vowel sonnet.

During the 1960s she took classes from Walter Van Tilburg Clark. He challenged and encouraged her—in both her poetry and her prose. His careful reading of her work during this period led to their long friendship. Though little of her prose was published, she wrote several short stories at different times throughout her life.

In 1962 de Longchamps taught a course on contemporary poetry at the University of Nevada, Reno. For the next ten years, she would continue teaching and lecturing intermittently at the university, culminating in her appointment as the first Walter Van Tilburg Clark Lecturer in Creative Writing at that campus in 1973.

That same year she wrote the lyrics for a symphony composed by Gregory Stone entitled "Reno, Fantastic Reno." It was performed by the Reno Philharmonic Symphony Orchestra at the Pioneer Theatre. Two years later she had an exhibition of her collages entitled "The

Naked and the Nude" at the Piñon Gallery in Reno (November 2–22, 1975).

When not writing, she devoted her life to the visual arts. In an interview conducted in 1980 with Jim McCormick and art critic Jeff Kelley, from which come many of the quotes in this biography, she told of gathering two hundred to three hundred pieces of paper before she began work on a collage, knowing "the pigment was fading as she glued them to paper." In another interview she said, "I do a great deal of research. . . . You can't write about a bat or produce the feeling of a bat unless you submerge yourself in the subject."

Her son Dare received his bachelor's degree in psychology from the University of California at Santa Cruz in 1971. He volunteered and worked in the mental health field before starting graduate school in 1975, majoring in psychology at Western Michigan University in Kalamazoo. Unhappy with the program, he returned home to live with de Longchamps at her Center Street house. Despondent, Dare took his own life at the Galena Creek house on January 27, 1976.

Ruth Cutten, who had been such a presence in de Longchamps's life, died in a Carson City nursing home in September 1982.

During the last ten years of her life de Longchamps battled multiple sclerosis and cancer. Determined not to paint "with a brush held in my teeth," her failing health became the subject of her posthumous manuscript *The Glass Hammer*. In 1983 she was conferred an honorary doctorate from the University of Nevada, Reno, and in that same year, received the Governor's Art Award in recognition of her significant contribution to literature in Nevada. After an acrimonious separation, she and Galen were divorced in 1983.

At her sixtieth birthday party, de Longchamps said to her good friend, Joan Arrizabalaga: "You better enjoy me now. I'm not going to have another birthday." Ms. Arrizabalaga recalled that de Longchamps had such strong beliefs, as if she could will herself to be in control of death.

De Longchamps held her last collage exhibition at the Sheppard Fine Arts Gallery in Reno from October 21 to November 15, 1983. This retrospective was the culmination of twenty-five years of work in the collage medium and is thought by many to be her most significant exhibition. Friends recall taking her to the opening. At that time she was using a wheelchair and felt uncomfortable in public, but she was truly honored to see so many close friends turn out for the opening.

On November 13, 1983, Joanne de Longchamps died of cancer at her house on Center Street. At her request, her ashes were scattered at Pyramid Lake (the following August).

People describe de Longchamps with many different terms: survivor, quick witted, and stunning. I would add to that list: sensual, disarmingly honest, bright to a fault, and motivated by a desire to "touch some lives" with her art. She loved the Great Basin, loved the air, space, and light in Nevada, and often compared it to Greece, saying she had only "felt air like this three times in her life": Pyramid Lake, Greece, and the airport in Honolulu. "There is a quality of air and light and movement of light and shadow that I saw in the Aegean that is [at] Pyramid Lake." A former student told of their talking about the light in Nevada for three hours while driving back from dinner in California. To another student she said: "You can come in (my poetry workshop) if you love poetry more than life itself." Intimidated, the student deferred and never took the class. An early acquaintance of de Longchamps described her this way: "Passionate in nature, she was not a knowable person." To Patty Atcheson, "she was a mentor," one who encouraged her to pursue watercolor portraits. And one of her dearest friends at the end of her life said, "She either loved you or didn't have time for you." Though these recollections seem discrepant, they accurately reflect her complexity as an artist and a person.

This collection of her poetry will, I hope, introduce new readers to a rare Nevada voice. Though she published seven books, and poems in *Poetry*, *Prairie Schooner*, *The New York Times*, *Poetry Northwest*, *The Antioch Review*, *American Scholar*, and *Southwest Review*, she remained virtually unknown out of the state: "Nevada hardly knows me as a poet." Her poem "Letters to Dare" appeared in a 1984 anthology edited by Greg Kuzma, *Poems for the Dead*, which included work from such poets as Richard Wilbur, James Wright, Philip Levine, A. R. Ammons, and others. She received several awards, among them the Reynolds Lyric Award in 1954, the *Carolina Quarterly* Award in 1959, and publication in the Borestone Mountain Poetry Awards Best Poems Series for four years. On October 13, 1989, she was inducted into the Nevada Writers Hall of Fame.

In Nevada she said, there is a "feeling of unity simply

because the land is so bare. . . . We're fed by our being hungry. And you do hunger in this state. You want some kind of a reaction and it's damn slow coming." And as if to reconcile her presence here, "You learn to live with the absolute elements." Not only did she learn to live with them, she recreated these absolute elements in her poetry and collage, leaving a legacy of light.

Shaun T. Griffin

Torn by Light

And Ever Venus
1944

Early Spring

These are the gray days, and the mournful sky
Has thrown a sullen glance along the earth;
Hushed are all footfalls, an impatient sigh,
The wind is keening with a winter mirth.
Gray as a dove-throat are these waiting days
That promise hyacinth and blade of green,
As if the silence in clandestine ways
Were hoarding loveliness we have not seen.
Locked in the moist dark sleeps the quiet seed,
Blossom in bud, the life-strength in deep root;
Sheltered in darkness from the frost's white greed
Is fiery flower and a golden fruit.

Denial

I love—in loving I was never wise,
And now your beauty is denied to me;
The steady glance of bold impassioned eyes,
Ten fathoms deep, and green-gray like the sea.
Your laughter, full and fertile in its mirth,
Yes, you are kin to elemental things
For it is rich and warm like this brown earth
Wherefrom the heavy-headed clover springs.
And I who knew rare wonder at your touch
Knew also that your restless blood ran flame.
How strange that I who felt love overmuch
Possess of you not one thing but your name.
Rich laughter, deep as earth, eyes like the sea,
The fires of your blood, denied to me.

LAT —
8-19-94
goodby my love.
Y B

3

Sonnet to a Husband

Say what you think—do what you will to me
But do it subtly, wrap around each word
A covering so that I may not see
In bold display the sharp gleam of a sword.
Be strong, demand—but do it gently so
That I may glory in my humbleness.
And never, my beloved, let me know
You take for granted one smile, one caress.
Be gay with me and love me as a child
As well as woman, for I know my heart
To be a fragile thing, afraid and wild.
I know it to be candid, without art.
Do this that I may lull myself to sleep,
In loving you—I have no wish to weep.

With Night Undone

In what words shall we talk of love
that has no longer
passion as an only child;
that breathes a secret life, stronger
than at first mating, calm yet wild?

Love, the shadow and the substance;
the night and noonday;
dark things and the light, merged one,
willed and unwilled—What shall we say,
with night and the sweet rites undone?

In what tongue shall we spell it out,
the Roman's best?
or wisely let your fingers speak
their silent message to my breast—
and know that all our words are weak?

Eden Under Glass
1957

Poor George, Everywhere

Contriving breasts shaped to hand's measure
you maunder mentally, fondling treasure;
caress love's loveliest sheathed by golden
smoothest softskin, shaped
to lust like a slipper.

Wived by woe to contemplate
love-lack house, hibernal bed, compensate
as girls go romping through your head;
are housed in dim apartments looking down
on secret streets of blue nocturnal town.

Race all your avenues and shivering pursue
staccato tap, tattoo of heels that quiver
ecstatic flank, eurythmic thigh—
No, not alone, your brothers burn
to seize a partner, prance a turn.

Tea-Time: Atomic Age

Afternoon. Create the delicate hours
with measured murmurs. Thrust thin towers
of conversation; white spires pricking air,
frail cities of sound, pale minarets,
ringed with the fine, dry mist of cigarettes.

Play piano, notes like apples, round
and firm with pink delicious sound
called wizardly from vast, invisible trees.
(Eclipse the vision of our bitter fruit,
wind-blasted orchard and the poison-root.)

Sip amber, plucking courage from a tray.
Speak love or art. Revive the wilting day
and close a quiet curtain to efface
impatient whines of anger, idiot-feet,
a monster loose along the peaceful street.

Grandmother and the Apple

Never again the lap,
widespreading cotton ledge of warmth,
or the incredibly soft, slack breast of age
pillowing the infanthead.

I cultivated nightmare,
screamed terror to the parlor
where rocking chair, iron stove
and grandmother creaked the time.

Here child, your feet are cold.
These nights are chilly, feeling better?
In her hand the fruit knife curved
and pounced upon the apple skin.

Thin steel hissed on fruit,
scraping applemeat to blade-tip.
Here my sweet, don't cut your lip.
Apple blood ran down my chin.

Obstetrician

Immaculate and smiling just enough:
(engender ease and not embarrass)
as hands are lively so his heart is tough.
Hands removed forever from that head
which smiles and speaks to obviate
probing questions in a sterile glove.
Impervious, the man of starch and steel
dominates and smiles, a man of charts
marking the whirlpools of a queasy course.
Facing birth's black core, the climax come—
after the longest day, a longer night,
dare to presume automaton made flesh.
Realities of pain and light obtrude.
Pits are plumbed singly. He whose smile is masked
attends our miracle and is unmoved.

Portrait: Housewife

She makes a fetish of her faithfulness,
whose private loathing is the double-bed;
a public symbol of the willingness
that, absent, breeds a halo for her head.
She spends bleak passion in domestic rites,
forcing a frigid pattern on the days
that corset conversation, appetites,
and leave her victim to a stern self-praise.
Existing in a chrysalis of fear,
the senses starve within a given space
and flirt with madness whose approach is clear . . .
Frustration trails a fist across her face.
She plans on heaven that will compensate—
a thousand grinning demons wink . . . and wait.

Jury Duty

The seldom-visitor to public buildings
learns the first hard lesson of its chairs,
needs patience in the drafts and weighty airs—
A citizen removed from secret self
discovers time is longer than he knew
as now, again, the trapped eye travels up
to march on molding, amble with the clock.
He may deplore the civic architecture
or walk the inner-maze of his conjecture.

But this is prologue: from the dusty branch
of unwished waiting springs our bud of doom,
like evil foliage tension grips a room.
This random audience off shoppers' street,
from workday dens or snug suburbia
is named and sworn, assembled to condemn;
presumed quite fit to cast a cutting stone.
We see the living half of death's duet
led out from cell to stony strangers' view.
He killed his wife—the matter rests with you.

But faces, O the faces disconcert,
no raveling these maskers for the thread
of what is hidden always in the head.
The judge more bland than any mandarin;
calm lawyers setting verbal chessmen out
are suave or strident in a planned intent
to checkmate. We confuse the king with pawn—

These witnesses are speaking as by rote.
If words are weapons honed to sever breath
how far this skillful play seems from a death.

An indoor drama has usurped a world
as seasons slide like leaves beneath our feet.
Unreal snowfall in the actual street
becomes but segment of a window-view.
Not under leafy silt or snow but speech
the days are drifted. Has a truth been sifted
or obscured beneath the long barrage?
The court reporter winds a mile of words:
the bailiff's gavel drives a nail of fear.
A verdict is one other word to hear.

Idyll

Our city plans for green escape
have seeded in a summer place—
Days curve like melons globing warmth
and gaping golden at the core.
We ask for more, forevers and not days
snatched from a season of indulgent weather
but idylls are brief and various.
We celebrate in lap of sun and lee of leaves.

By word and touch a planet spins,
precarious as Eden under glass.
Its growing light, swelling the membrane of memory,
outshines known worlds, familiar and now far.
Our questions are sad and curious—
Where else will morning dark with trees
be pierced by slanting thorns of light,
reveal the early roses of the day?

Already we project to colder time
and reconstruct the lived-in now,
translating act to legend, kiss by kiss.
We raise that solitary edifice,
the sealed museum in a lover's head
to house in bone the burning souvenirs.
Side by side beneath the willow's cover
sweet, warm, close, we grieve each for the other.

The Sea Outlasts the Summers

I   *The Window*

Hotels can be haphazard heavens,
their cells with dust or honey lined—
Beyond those casual curtains all night long
the sea, insomniac, droned song.
Stars, moon dissolved at midnight like a wish,
like ghosts of wishing saltfog slipped the sill
followed by a hoarse and solemn horn
that speaks to warn.

. . .

Matisse felt this moment
painting the sight
of windowed sea—His woman stands
in a morning light.
As one who wakes from love
her pose is slack.
Rising, she pauses, lost to water view
before his urgent arms cajole her back.

II   *The Pier*

All things these waters touch are close to grief,
even this summer instance drugged with light
has surface shimmer only. Yellow and brief
the season of sun is simple varnishing

for the cold kept under, the colors kept
in shifting layers angled from our sight.
We look and say, the sea is green today.

We look and walk in love along the pier,
warm with each other, my hand inside your hand,
and move into the sideshow atmosphere
of booths with shoddy flags, the diving bell.
Our joy flings out to race the whirligigs
but carnivals are spinning in your hand
where private music turns a carousel.

Subtract from days and sullen nights to live
this time together. Shadows on a scene
of staying sea we play the fugitive
and move to shoals of loss. The cutting reef
of forced goodbyes warns shipwreck, will destroy
this more-than-pleasure craft, love's brittle boat.

All things that lovers touch are close to grief.

III   October

Inland the Autumn verticals intrude—
bird up, leaf down.
The strict year in its shattering is hazed,
here filmed light builds metallic monuments
of bronzed trees, pasturelands of brass.

Who walks the horizontal shore,
pacing the pier and passing

the shuttered hexagon that houses
painted horses static in their stalls?
The silvered swan won't glide again this year.

What stranger in fogged afternoon
hears the wooden echo of his steps
and pauses in the shelter where we paused?

The wind assaults
whose litter is not leaves but paper summer
blown on the boardwalk, harried out
and splayed on rusting rails or spiralled down
to lasting sea where every season drowns.

Subzero Letter

No golden girls in costly diapers
lounge here, my curious love.
This is a cold country,
removed by time and bleak geography
from all our sun and neon littered lives;
pool pleasures, Pacific attitudes.

Here cold is tangible; kicks, clings,
rears to strike from every cornerstone.
But you are safe; sun-comforted
and couched on sand, your burnished head
stopping the mouth of quiet wind.
(I see you so, filling those sandy valleys
with small and tender mountains of your breast.)

Believe me, winter is more than words,
more than landscapes crouching under snow.
Only the heart is safe and will not freeze . . .
This is a cold country:
Wait for me.

Words Under Rain

Not you, not I
on this shaken gourd-globe
churning persistent seeds at the candent core,
will be remembered.

No longer recalled than rain
whose anonymous fall
spills unpresaged by personal thunder.

What the mind can keep is briefly safe,—
and ardors;
time-capsuled, stinging, separate,
are points of sand
pearl-coated by inaccurate memory.

What stays but probing the doubtful dream
that fails with you
or dissipates with me?

ws
9/20/94

Act III, Scene III

Ten years removed from fabled afternoons
and lovers' circumstance we drift
in conversation clinking over spoons,
hollow as common cups we lift
and settle roundly in saucer rings.

(Invaded, we are summered with soft wings
that hover the source of memory,
seek vanished warmth, enclosing bough,
the leaf-locked shelter of nesting tree,
lost orchards magicked into now.)

As waiters hum and move among their plates
we sit apart and speak. Silence waits
finale for façade of words
raised to a season blood recalls
in imagery of wings—These lurching birds
flail out against us and the tower falls.

Feathers spinning on our lips and eyes
obscure the waiters, bowing, as we rise.

Tango

Our longest love will not outlive us
but go down crying in the cold
of those sealed countries walled within.

Heat dictates the tango years
and we outlive our gliding loves,
outstay our spring and summer selves
repenting of the coldest change
when forward looking turned its face
to looking back.
                          See
all our moons ascend and snap
like children's lost balloons of light.

Over meadows moulting down,
hot landscapes alter to a thin
God-fearing city spiked with spires,
robbed of roses and of swans.

Rivers carried prints of leaves,
sucked sweetness in a riot of sun
where ice has settled down to stay—
trees are gallows waving ghosts.

There is nothing to be done but this:
Take grief to bed, last chilly lover
who will be faithful kissing in the cold.

Moment Musicale

Give me a hundred sounds for stillness.
Lip me a song with slow vowel tones.
Work up a fine marimba frenzy,
tickle the long rib bones.

Straddle a cello, make it grumble.
Rattle a gourd with seven seeds.
Grind on a gilded hurdy-gurdy.
Pipe on three hollow reeds.

Zither or banjo, balalaika,
archlute, mandora, samisen—
Capable instruments of pleasure
where are the music-men?

Where are the dapper concertmasters?
Where are the leaders of the bands?
(Leaving me hostage to the silence,
clapping my empty hands.)

Island, Island

Morning, the sunstruck sea circling and sighing
urged us to island, buoyed the bright boat.
We rowed over singing—
a simple remove from mainland to rock
and beached on fair sand.
The weekday invasion of Sunday shore
intruded on somnolence:
city-white satyrs and pale secretaries
altered to Adam, fugitive Eve.

Mystery moved us veering as mist moves
and lifts—undulant yellow tides
gilded our swimmers.
Poised in shallows sieved by seaplants
we dreamed salt spectrum, layered light;
green in blue and merging rose
that plunges purple to no-color dark.
Above us gulls scythed acres of sweet air.

Warmed by windless afternoon
we picnicked and parted—amorous twos
seeking the spiral course of pleasure,
pinkconed shells circled on sand.
These and a white quill, boneshard and pebble
signalled our solitude, spoke love.
Daylong we lingered nourished by the sun
that sparked an early star before it downed.

Leaving was losing Eden, habit-flight.
Unhoused by simple sorrow we rowed out,
feeling at our backs the island-arc
diminish like a moon to be remembered.

Exitus

Wind that blew a world away
revisits on the shrinking stone,
dogwind sniffing moonish dust;
untenanted, sans movement, all.
No steely ganglia where cities stood
before their discus flight on space
and nowhere watersound or shine
but grotto-dark, a deadstar fruit.

A world well lost?
and not for love
whose lack envenomed air,
tossed toadstooled murder planetwards.
By harvest is the tree's strength known—
time's yield of cankered wormwound fruit
snapped logically from universal bough.
The serpentshape was man.

Who, remembering, laments
earth's green experiments;
mourns the body's logos torn
out of context, chaos-caught,
or sees, dispersed in thin insentient space
the templed architecture of sweet bones?
A child there was that blew in beauty down.

Wind that blew a world away
circles thrice on spinning stone
before the final outer fall,
blind fragment thrown.

Void, a settling shade
and day dead
green and growth gone
deed, desire done
sound and sweet spent
wind and world blown—
World there was
that spun in darkness down.

Advice to the Life-Lorn

Now is a ripe orange. Seize, love it—
Fondle, maul, tease-torture,
Lips, teeth, tongue, tender and violent.

Orange my sum and symbol of
everything with juice in it,
each dripping hive.

Apples in our orchards of goodbye
pucker and twist,
withered faces, little antique moons.

Now is your orange,
flesh sweating sweetness.
Ten thousand drunken pores suck air and light.

Time is frost, both early and late,
and the crashing bough.
Take Now.

Tourist in the Temple

Greece is cool in the mind—
a green phrase uttered as islands.
Birds bridge them, doves and destroyers,
salacious gods in swan's guise—
(conjuring Leda, envy her
moved in such whiteness).

Myth-mating gods we remember,
confuse them with place
as the mind's airy map rejects fact.
We choose a statue's bled stone
to the dark, living face.
Greece is a garland, a word
in a white ring of columns.
This Greece never happened—
no age was so classically golden,
so heavy with hyacinths.

Circling stalks of unpetalled stone
we dream a false flowershape
romantic in ruin.

Fugue

Again a stricken season alters us,
shocking the summerselves with antic wind;
a scythe for burnished days, the furious
flail on livid treescape—siphoning veins,
stripping the mind's warm branches of their fruit,
lashing at leaf and love with rapier rains.

Winter is a jealous season, frustrate,
lapping burial linens over land
that bred blue lilac, lilies, and the late
tightbudded tawny crushed chrysanthemum.
Huddle within walls feeding garnet flame
that bleeds slow roses—and remember them.

Blackbird Tree

In far fields white in winterlock
(the keys, the cold seeds underground)
stripped and single appletree
visited with sudden sound

is shivered trunk and narrow branch,
set shaking with a blossoming
of blackest birds, of beaky buds
obsidian petalled wing on wing

poised as flowers over boughs
but vocal as no flowers seen
lamenting lack of leaves, complaint
for gathered fruit and vanished green—

this feathered foliage scatters up
impossibly, as leaves must fall—
the whitest silence rushes back
and that is all and that is all.

Snowmountain

From valley floor and smokestack town
we came to this mountain dimension,
the cold fact of winter as eye would have it
in white script, a fable of snow
alive with groved aspen, grave pine
in each part burnished and blazing.

Clean here; high bright precipitous
and struck with pure sunfall.
Our tears glaze the dazzlement:
lungs test the knives of the air
and blood's small warmth, our animal fire
seems threatened. We crouch in our bones.

Soundless down vertical acres
a skier drops like a spider, spins out
sudden tracks in a web of descent.
He has skimmed the new cream of the snow
and released us, glossed over the menace,
crossed over the sheer malevolent mountain.

The warm dumb beast that cowers in blood
sensed death in alpland. But we are saved
by the way a landscape alters with figures,
is reduced to a backdrop. We seem to conquer—
This motion restores us: motion the catalyst
changing the primitive pause of fear
to sudden joy. We shout to the mountain.

The Hungry Lions
1963

Echoes from the Playground

Complex now the simple hide-and-seek
that matched its running length against the dark,
shutting out the bedtime faces
that frowned me from my pleasure.
From hiding, I seek in colder light,
minus the shout and stripped of glee
and all that were out are not in free.

Gritty squares and stick-drawn circles
framed my rude geometry of joy.
Hopping from cube to cube, a one-leg stagger
foretold a later stance:
indecision's dance, the too-short leap
could lock me in the enemy's square,
and boundaries, I found, were everywhere.

Inside the lines of coloring-books
or jumping loops of moving rope
I was magic-ringed, child of peripheries,
wishing a world of safe circumference
yet danger-drawn, an acrobat of fences
who dared abyss, defied the sidewalk crack
that waits to break a mother's back.

Menaced, I fled to secret zones,
to daydream's beckoning "King's X"
that has, at first and last, the form of love.
Gathering tricks and talismans
I was sorceress of sticks and stones
with a finger-cross for the fatal lie—
but crossing my heart, I never hoped to die.

Between the City Gates and the Sea

Late scholar of my own despair
I breathe an air alive with omen
yet grieve at a change
when every child in a flowery town
knows ashes, *ashes all fall down*—

dry rain of ash made metaphor
for the sudden personal Pompeii.
Runners from that fiery fall
were found cast down in ash. Daily we flee
between the fire and the sea.

Unmoving, the desperate flight unmade,
death will invade by ingrown weather.
Now test the twins of choice;
return's slim chance and the bitter breaking
if every road leads to leave-taking.

In sulphurous light, sense ash and cinder,
the fall of small and scorching stones.
Will my bones be found
with the cowards crushed in their cellar-holes,
crouched over jewels and shattered bowls?

A hero travels his brave bloodstream,
Himself the city and sea of dream.

Widow's Song

A young man so fair
can shed a blaze of blondness
on the darkest bed
and suggest blanched stone or star
in a far frieze of sky,
yet be warm—as the living are.

I think: I am touching smoke
or a pearl of cloud
in a dalliance with lesser jewels,
for where that flesh lies thin,
a pulse beats green,
jade in the startling skin.

So fair, newcomer, stranger,
white-gold where a swarthy ghost
still spurs me from his dark.

I come to you from one
who made warm lairs for me, long years
I wintered in black fur.

A White Zone of Death, of Dream

See how I rouse and move to morning
like Alice out of wonder's underground,
but Alice older, deciphering her dreams.
Through mirrors of green ice,
from cinemas and sad charades of sleep
I have come back
to still another waking at your side.

I dreamed the colors of the cold
locking a captive snowqueen in a sleigh
drawn by white horses. Everywhere
snow spun and settled in a sleepy light
and brushed a further white on the running mares
whose hoofbeats made their music twice—
once in echo, once on ice.

Think that white sleigh drawn on white
that fanned a spray of jade,
and I, a cold queen, looking down
from frozen fountains the runners made
to see a monster fish beneath that ice
whose black fins swept in pace
with the racing sleigh.

Green ice held and the great fish followed under,
a first, not a final shape of fear.
From nowhere, from spinning ground

a deeper shadow veered
and white air belled with sound.
Wild dogs of wasteland bayed for death,
a lean pack slanted over snow,
black on the dreamer's track.

Warm lovers should be first to know
opposing colors of the cold
and how the dark pack runs beside
and the black shape swims below.

A Way of Traveling

Love is not a resting place,
lover is not crutch or mirror.
Private body and public face
divide their terror.
One hides, one smiles,
they are steplocked and crazed.
How endure, unpropped,
be beautiful, unpraised?

Fear the touch of give
that stretches to receive,
then in dual lovelessness
head and body grieve.
They must be one or perish,
for flesh will kindle face,
and head instruct the body
to a moving grace.

If easy in a single skin
for spending or taking,
grasp courage to begin
love's rousing and slaking.
Strong without a crutch,
fair without a mirror,
discover self to other,
both gift and giver,

and so move doubly-warm
and need no resting space.

Love, a way of traveling
beyond a given place.

One Definition of a Clown

The selves in self plot civil wars,
ready wranglers, rude in their embrace.
If each desire had bone and face,
welled blood would stifle into scars,
but familied in a single fort
brutes and darlings bruise each other.
Do-good scolds the ape's bright brother.

Peace is the grave's word, we speak it gravely,
infatuate with angels, harped and haloed
and blind to sweetly muscled fact:
we are malformed for airy diving
out or down to voids of calm,
here or in a heaven-space.
Poor sad-in-self, embalming views,
glass-belling love and place.

But the passage of windy years breaks glass.
The tragedy and music of our grief
falls on the obdurate hard hide of things
like shattered wind-chimes, simple clink and tinkle,
our dirge for drums, an aria for bells—
this makes us clown, a chalk-faced irony.
We add the clown, persona to the plot
that is ourself, a clown both ape and angel.

Old Man Singing at the Edge of Land

I sunned the heavy breast beneath my hand.
My spider-mother gave warm milk and later
I tore the web to find a new equator.
Egypt I held sinning at my side,
spun new myths with an old spell
and took a lioness as bride,
proving the forms the mind can marry.

I lusted more than I could carry,
found wenches in books, round girls in galleries,
and forged my role on wayward histories
in fantasy before the fact.
Early, late and no longer,
I starved and sang toward the double act.
Why does an old man sing? I sing to die.

At land's blue margin sirens ply
grim shuttles for all shapes that move—
I use my breath to bargain with,
to trade for healing death those heats of love.

Reunion

Here in a livingroom of ever after
we meet, adults, and strangely stranger-cousins
alien out of childhood's sealed retreat.
Words are slow self-conscious commentary
until the key "do you remember?" turns
and gently pries a gilded door of Christmas . . .

Yearly to the tall house flanked by gum trees
and a remnant orchard brittle in December,
my father, prodigal, made pilgrimage
back to the lonely nest: an only son
he shone a ruddy-golden as they gathered,
the meager clan of proper Scots, dour
except for Grandpa, silver-maned and massive,
who dealt his blacksmith pinches out of love.

Flat-footed, Grandma paced from stove to sink
in an endless meal chain, smiling long-lipped smiles,
her eyes grown sadly huge behind thick lenses.
A daughter bustled near, the nervous mother
of this one who says, "do you remember?"
and maiden great-aunts (papery lips and hands)
emerge. Great doors slide, booming in their grooves
and parlor time begins: blue cut-velvet sofa,
geometric doilies, looming photographs
of the decent dead exhumed by conversation
that was a feat of things not said, evasions,
clauses of omissions that denied
the family problems, drink and diabetes.

We, restless children itching for an exit,
wound the vast victrola, thump and squeak,
(Maxwelton's braes were bonnie for a week)
or escaped to iceland in an outdoor closet
with revealing water-roar and link-chain rattle,
crouched to a knothole in the backporch boards
with nothing to see but thrifty rows
of frosted fruit, the last blood-oranges picked
whose fragrance was identified with cold.

Or daring the certain scold-tongues crept inside
a lair of spiders, climbed black pumproom stairs
under a listless winter windmill, older
than the elegant fashion-ladies out of print,
tacked, bustle and boa to the rounded walls.
We talked there in forbidden whisperings
about unsteady uncles; Bert who had a bathhouse
remembered from a single summer day—
recalled his rheumy eyes and nickel gifts
and hot dogs—revived the magic smell
of brine under the sand-sharp slatted walkways
that led to gritty cubicles. Ancient bathing caps,
ear-plugs and eye-shades laced with rancid oil
were shelved in dusty graveyards for dead flies.

Guilty and grinning we left, revived the dead victrola.

At last the weighty supper was put down
and gathered evening reddened the stove's paned eye
that winked a warmth on evergreen indoors.
Santa was Uncle Jack with bridle bells

rung in the waiting stillness after dark.
Then, *then* the presents and "do you remember?"
sadly the last lost domino was found
and dry night kisses doled out by the aunts
after Grandpa's hearty tweak and smack.
Then only bed was left in upstairs arctic,
toe-torturing icefloe sheets. Warmth disappeared
at the first stair-landing where a loosened board
bleated in the chill. We paused then passed
the painting of a life-size paper boy
whose brush-stroke tears held halfway down his cheek
for the unsold papers named *Examiner*.

Doors close on children, on the stranger-friends.
Cousin, goodnight and come again, again.

A Minor Venice Painted on the Summer

Sea that threshes bone of bird and tumbles stone
moves on the land like sleep
in retreat before returning.
I move downsand as to a sleep of pleasure,
entreating the dream for something warm,
potion that saves or tropic of elation,
and reach the cold commotion of the waves,
a chill coast done with burning.

Beach to boardwalk points a flimsy town,
flying port of stilts and wheels
where plaster palaces of fun
paint a minor Venice on the summer;
carnivals of moving towers
in a water-park of piers,
those dead trees planted down
that wear the bluer bark of barnacles.

Two seastruck lovers
lived over a carousel,
tethered to their tower
like clappers in a bell—
Swung above a stable
where stallion, lion and swan
wheeled afternoon to evening
in a carved continuum.
Underfoot and overhead
lurched to the prancing,

moved the lovers in their bed
to a double dancing—
and they believed the fable
of the gilt harmonium.

Poem, the artifact of love,
is scooped from wintering sand,
a stone still warm from summer.
And sea that reaps the brittle bones of birds
moves on the land like sleep
teaching the watercolored words,
although they rave of wheels and towers,
to dance to graver music with the waves.

Ask Why I Dream

Ask why I dream of seaweed money
and a rocking chair that sings and cracks.
Of all the worlds that weave me in
I am unwound by looking back.

In dark down-city Sunday dreams,
ships founder in the watery parks
and spill the sprawling night-sea crews
where I must walk on shores of stone
to meet the dandy of my childhood
rocking in his broken shoes;
rocking man of lullabies
who blew me down with song
and pumped to break the rocker's back.

Those were the tides I moved along
to warmest latitudes of sleep
who pace this stranger on the street,
my dancing father, heel and toe,
doing a sailor's reel in space
and the city decks unsteady.

A voyage flickers on his face,
the thousand waves that sped him here
and the north star lost so early.

There are no words that we can sing.
There is this dark place where we stand.
He drops the anchor of his hand
into a pocket's puzzle,
and the diving hand is strong
that pulls up scant, sad weeds of money
and holds them out to me like song.

Delivered from a Heaviness of Love

—delivered from a heaviness of love,
released by time in abstract act of death—
The subtle burden pledged was light as lyric
altered from soft beginnings to a stone.

To be removed from luckless love,
the ruse of romance and its forced recall,
is to return by marvel to go forth.
Who should foretell that vivid lines
shall plod dull rhythms to their ruin?
Now stripped of sentimental vines,
walls disappear, leaving us with light
in open acres. Our sad remains are air.

If empty shell were sentient, by a trick
could feel a sea invasion on high realms
of vacant coil and curve, could sense the free
and saltsweet wash and hammock rock of wave
that buoys and bears from here to other where
this, then, is how to be in interim; weightless,
out of love and loveless, briefly spent
and richly far from bodies of our grief.

Cellar Bar

Moving in the sapphire dusk of bars,
let down on ropes of need, let down again
to caves of glancing glass and dancing ice,
pretend explorer, strike safari pose
and seek from eye's sly corner a reflection
more brave, more beautiful than we will ever be.

Pretend and then extend the imagery
to round these others shadowed in thick smoke
as if each inhalation promised love
or golden medals for their swift descent.
Cave-comrades all, a coed clan subterre,
pitching tilted tents of fur and blur.

The scene needs music, let a sad bass warn
perpetual pathos to the happy horn
muted in a pause when strangers kiss.
But touch is flare, pinpointing on abyss,
a random lantern swung on swaying night—
so much of lack revealed by such small light.

A Further Dialogue for Clowns

This is the day the self divides
and mind takes sides—
flesh says *fly,* uneasy on its bones
cries *out* and *go*—but the day,
dismally set for dialogue,
bids body stay

as mind revolves on discontent,
for being greedy yet afraid
of mirrors, movement, change—
it grabs to hold and hoard,
and if arrangements shift,
jumps to rearrange

and catches on the dream of pride,
those fabled roles assigned inside,
each one heroic in its ease,
paced to please and for applause.
The private dramas fail
but self will circle on their flaws,

considering a fate of fools
and inadvertent clowns
abused with laughter, bruised by falls.
The fictions of perfection bear
no clutching at preposterous pants
or pride caught in its underwear.

Clown inside, you are my fear
as I endure a captive child,
the fatal whisper in my ear:
Be good, be brave, be beautiful
and everyone will surely love you—
advice impossible to prove
even if true.

Lines for Late Spring

How faithful to love when lovers lose
by further faithfulness to love
and freshness fails? The sweetest jails
are built for love, the narrowest bed
grows wide to span a wealth of dread
and discontent is duly sheathed
in daily acts of learned benevolence.

Beginnings bred a sweeter violence—
bubble-Parnassus where we grew to gods—
undoing in single nights the guardian net
our mortal mothers lifelong wept to weave.
Tamed, we tie the careful knots again,
proud or shamed by a shadow presence
sheer at our side. We name the tall ghost love.

We need too much, are greedy for opposites.
Given a grove to glide as nymphs,
a hearth with children haunts the revel
and we fathom too late a family beast
grown docile for the brood and board.

The crux of jest is time. The luckiest nymph
has outlived love or is a legend, dead,
or yet discovers on her joggling breast,
grizzled and friendly, an aging satyr's head.

A Mathematic of Change

1 . . . Saint Mary's Hospital

Beneath the portico at 4
pass bronze Mary in her niche
and give to her the summer light
that leaves you at the entrance door.
Down anterooms of smoke,
in rows of captive faces
watch a small boy, wildly bored,
hop in metal braces.
With you on the waiting-chair
is flash-fright, wing in the gut.
Feed with dwindling crumbs of hope
the blacker birds of fear
and jump to hear a spoken name,
(I move so far from what was me).
In triplicate for twenty minutes
formalize a malady
to walk a hall at 5 o'clock,
child of fury to be there,
punished for obscure defects
and sent to bed without your supper.

You find a narrow locker, numbered,
a scrubbed side-table, neat,
that holds a polished pitcher and a glass.
The crank-up bed has a rubber sheet.

2

By deft degrees the senses slip
and drift, deprived of panic—
by sleeping pill the night before
and morning hypodermic.
Shifted to a stretcher-bundle,
trundled down a drunkard's night,
rouse once before the gasping sleep,
strapped in a closing trap of light.

Brusque, a mittened movement at my head.
When did the echo say: *her hair is red*.

3

From anesthetic dream
I flew and fell on two round words
too great for me to hold,
spoken from the swimming dark:
mimosa, marigold.

Heard, not seen, two floating forms
made their meaning as I roused
and altered into image, told
themselves in repetition, were
mimosa, marigold;

a yellow shine, dim suns
or sparks and spinning coins
knotting on the clotted cold,

joining me to flowering light:
mimosa, marigold.

4

The amputee will sing a song:
"There are two selves where I was one."
We will use my given name
to clothe an optimist,
a jokester lately and a lover
and have no telling title for
this new and curious cipher
in a cancer-mathematic,
sprung from a rib of pain
and prone to panic.
Regard me, sirs and stoic surgeons,
we have contrived a clever pair
from what was simply one,
and now, deliberate schizophrenic!

5

Four pillows; two large,
one at the head of a tilted bed
the other a boulder under knees.
Two small;
for the neck's hot hollow
and to brace a shoulder.

In a glass, cracked ice
making the simplest kind
of song against the spoon,

roaring around my teeth
as the jaws grind.

6

How relieved they are,
my family and friends
to hear me laugh, look,
propped and posed there
beside the rigid floral sprays
(carnation, gladiola, rose),
she makes a joke.

I laugh for him,
my wild and household love
who smiles to hear me laugh.
But that deep-falling glance,
grown wise to change,
will break, shatter askance.
We cannot dare a meeting of the eyes.

7

I have known it,
that burst of elation
to hear of someone's sickening,
car-wreck or cancer, love or death-loss,
that tiny rocket of relief
the self sends up,
saying: it was not I,
congratulations to me, three cheers,
look, *I am here*.

After, close after
the self's sustaining caper,
gasp in disbelief,
tears and terrors later.

Sweet bedside visitors,
bearers of cologne and flowers,
books and bangles, magazines,
I salute that first response,
accept your gifts with grace and irony,
knowing they are libations to the gods of grave
   mischance
and protect you more than they can comfort me.

8

On the wall brass Christ four inches long
is fixed by a prong to polished wood—
looking, I look away.
Feeling strong, I tour in slippers
and find a crucifixion down the hall—
this chromium Christus, *art-nouveau*,
is slick, a graceless figure.
Returning to my cubicle,
I look and like my brass Christ better.

9

The self-in-dream yet moves
serene in the known sweet
wholeness of flesh and loves,

meets the in-spun circumstance
of sleep and is complete.

Grief cometh in the morning,
grief will strike across
the light-borne morning, light renew
discoveries of loss.

10

False-simple the swift solution
drawn to a decision: *not to live,*
this resolution to refuse.
With liar's pride I plan my suicide,
rehearse by many methods death,
embrace it as a frantic lover
and put myself to sleep again
with tales of swart revolvers.

11

The Irish saved me,
the rich brogue burning
on ground-mists of gray morning
where the stiff, night-fallen trees
lie, lopped branch and bleeding bark,
undone again by dream and dark.

Druid, darling, angel of starch
moving through the morphine trees
with hands of warm and reddened leaves

to bring me honeywords and coffee
brewed to banish demons, hot as home.

Once through thin partitions
my sibyl spoke a spell
that propped me from the toppled dead:
Sure and that girl has guts she said.

12 . . . Talking to the Sun, Mid-August

Too weak to stand
against your heavy mid-day hand,
I take my morning coffee where you stroke
an early light along the lofts and leaves.

Awkward and unbeautiful
pale traveler to summer,
I have returned and turn
without all words to warmth—
and still a word must spell
the answer to my need: *impartial*.

If I say your hand strokes leaves
or your great eye scans the eaves,
it cannot change your vast uncaring
mindlessness that spins me free.
No judge of beauty or its lack,
you shine. If I am here beneath
you shine for me.

The Wishing Animal
1970

A Defense of Masks

Infants and animals
may go without disguise;
children snug in flawless skins,
beasts made to match the woods they're in—
or do I lie?
Veils conceal and baffle
in every set of eyes.

Innocence was armor.
Stripped, I praise pretence
and pride, a straight spine later on
for ignorance and beauty gone.
Add wit to sense,
gild and bedeck—or face
the truth of consequence.

Masks are needed, vizors,
dominos of daring;
a thousand tricks played to survive
the hazards if you stay alive,
the lessenings,
the long Lent of old age.
Go masked, give grace to mourning.

Do queens flap empty sleeves?
Decency dissimulates.
Beggars showing wounds for alms
find thinnest silver on their palms—
As candour sates,
illusions nourish.
Go gold, outdazzle fate.

Grimdeath and the Bones

Lovers die but caution kills
the living while they move
for Grimdeath marks the prudent bones
of puritans to make fine dice,
knowing virtue's ivory
is neatest formed for vice,
being upright, stiff and thin
from bearing little more than skin.

The bones of lovers have so burned
beneath the glowing flesh
turning in those fragrant fires,
that they are worthless to Grimgambler
who damns them to a garden
where the shed skin of a snake
loops across dead applewood
together with a muddied feather
trampled where a jealous angel stood.

Married

Not in a firm-fleshed beginning
are love's disguises known.
The tentative reachings,
the delicate first sorties of sense
speak only of themselves.
New lovers think they think alone;

are wise to shun the eyes of wedding guests,
of couples long-married, watching,
wanting to laugh and cry,
who have worn the secret masks
or refused them, and either way
known *love* was the burden they carried.

To the discipline of marriage,
the lesson shaped to a wing or cage,
they brought a stubborn caring, a courage
to find in strokes of surprise
the wish *not* to be parted, in spite
of all counter-wishing, in spite of rage:

found love was one child of anger,
grown strong in argument,
and words a way to learn the other,
a return to the fact and the act of love
when indifference threatened, when silence
poisoned the will's intent.

Love has risked itself to live—
for private nourishment
has dreamed the known flesh strange
and kindled love with faithlessness:
in a lawless and a legal bed
fed fantasies of license.

A live thing breeds in dark,
untouched, out of all sight,
seeds in seasons underground.
Seeking the why of marriage,
a black doubt stokes desire
yet our prayers cry to the gods of light.

A bride adjusts her veil: the veil is white.
The married couples watch together,
aware of pit and pinnacle. Two there
like ancient lovers; Baucis, Philemon,
wish death at the same instant, that not one
should leave before the other.

The Net-Menders

. . . for an anniversary

I speak a marriage metaphor,
of two who choose one strip of shore
for harbor;
              magnets, one to other
in their patterns of return,
tides tied to a moonclock;

of two in time, who are variously
the boat, the net, the sea
and the fleeing fish endlessly taken
that wriggles free to be caught again:

of two whose pleasure bends them
to the tedious mending of nets.

(Cold mariners unlearn the truth
that lovers hold: worlds end.
I dream a solitary swimmer
predestined to go down
those sheer and waterfalling stairs
where ships like sticks were snapped and drowned
before the earth became a round.)

And in your every absence I descend.

And I would swim beneath your keel,
a racing shadow that describes the day
as your nets create my sportive sea.

I would be the gleaming catch you angle for
and the tugging shores of your return.

My love, I know no more of love to say.

The Wind-Gardener

Summer boarders at sea-border
share the view with strangers.
Coming early from the beach
with a catch of shells, I watch
a blind man greet the morning.
He stands mid-garden, turning
and turning his face to meet the wind
and the fog-fed flowers in their colors
are colorless to him;
red, a dead language
but rose and geranium
are read as fragrance, brailles of scent.
A blind man reads the air,
aware of nothing in my place
and watching him, I disappear
as leaf and petal, sight unseen.
He turns and turns his face,
sharing no view with strangers;
a gardener of wind who gathers
essence of invisibles,
most secret rose and green.

To Harold

—who in dreams is visitor
and does not speak but leans
against me (companionable shoulder),
I turn, trusting the probing eye
and the proven love that bends
its listening to hear me.

In narrow dark-rooms, night
will print wry photographs that day,
filtering light, shuttering circumstance,
snapped when the wakened I
was inattentive to futures, doing
some usual thing, dressing or eating.

Some part of me keeps meaning clear:
Sleeping I see him; distanced, he is near.

A Singing

I praise
the song below
the surface

as I would sing
bones
shaping flesh

as I remember
sounds that were
curse and music
of a cure

as now I hear
their metal echo;
whisper
of the wizard-knives

that sang, that sang
my sleep below:

    We make your wounds,
    we steal your grace,
    we take your loves

to keep your life—
and flesh withdrawn
behold the bone
and warm beneath
another song;
the blood,
the bonny blood
sings on.

Hospital Visit

. . . for Elizabeth Bliss

I wait where schedules are coldly familiar;
where hours are patterns and time is a tailor
of shapeless shirts and spotless sheets
precisely tucked to their corners.
I listen to shuffling calendars;
the torn-off, hidden days of the years
since I willed my life away from here
in the burning name of light,
with a vow of no-return.
The voice of this day says: *not the same,*
now you wait upright as a visitor,
as friend, as other—and I remember
how love's stubborn soldiery wars on fear.

Moved from deep, far regions of sleep,
my friend who mumbles of monstrous dreams,
gropes from her sterile cave of cloth
to discover my hand and sleep again.
I shift my weight on a straight-backed chair.
I almost sleep in the even air
but a scissoring schedule cuts out a clock
to deliver a nurse with a fever chart
and I wake in the shock of her stare,
a stranger appraised in her guardian gaze
who is not remembered, not recognized.
I will it so. I would not be known.
There is little in common

with what she sees and a sunbrowned wanton
she attended and mended in quiet ways.
Belonging to then, I leave her there,
brushing red lengths of heavy hair,
lifting its tangle to cooler pillows,
her coming and going confused with stars.

Refusing the steep, backward step to her,
I refuse the one that she has forgotten
who left to become what I am, another;
a woman upright at a friend's bedside,
a stranger who feels her features harden
as if flesh, at last, would turn to stone
carved in a curved archaic form;
the forever-fixed face of Egypt,
the smile that decorates tombs.

A Bedlam Story

I knew a gray and only son
who had a lonely mother
and was driven near to terror
by her widow's tics and talks.
He saved and paid the going rate
of dollars for an hour
to be smiled upon and told:
"Talk is tonic for the old,
just pretend to listen
and let her ventilate."

Ah, the long, late windiness,
that vapid ventilation.
He thought she was an ancient fan
wheeling on his ceiling
in a chilling use of air.
And with telling and re-telling
of the past, she took the future
from a patient man pretending
that he wasn't there.

Found, Lost

I am a woman no longer young,
but what gray man is this
who praises reunion?

We pace a meadow, on and under green,
a lover's setting spaced with birds.
I hear my voice, girlishly high
in a singsong chirp and chattering.

Absence should claim and keep us
or desire grant its silence,
allowing the body to speak
a braille of signs,
to describe in moving lines
bridge, cave, fountain:
images acted upon.

Pebbles roll beneath our shoes,
wings cross-cut air;
and like a bored and boring child
trailing on a nature-walk,
I talk,
pointing a finger there and there,
asking the names for things.

A Masque of Meanings

The witch of birth touched my lips
a tap of forgetfulness.
Loosed from a nine-months' journey
I arrived one memory less,
beginning, then, at a loss;
and the breastwarm dark is gone,
the buoyant passage from arm to arm,
love looking down.
How long the circling finger poised
to buzz on dimple, navel, knee,
descending, being bumblebee?

With hive and honey gone,
Sister, Self, what have we done
for sweet or shame,
hands and heartbeats since
but seek our vanished name?
Turning in time as a figure
lost in a chamber of mirrors
looks out and is reflected back;
moving space as a dancer
spins for a circle of eyes,
changed in the thoughts of the watchers
to become her own disguise.

Lovers lift a faulty mirror;
look deep, the gentle glass will break
and the mended silver keep its seams.
Take an image from the shards
and rise to greet a stranger
or cross the timeless time of sleep,
eyes shut in dreaming's second-sight
to find once more
the thread that leads us into light
is fastened in a cave of water
and the green pools give our image back.

Wake and seek: a sky has no reply.
The birds sing to their own,
the leaves translate the wind
yet beauty gives and takes our breath.
The selves seal in their mysteries,
a secret honey swells the hive
and loves are bees that bring the sweet
for journeys that the living make.
A voice has said: "Your names
are many as a world of eyes
and when the witch-death seals your lips
and gives to bone its shirt of stones,
though stars and meanings cross,
you leave your wisdom to the wind
and end is as beginning, at a loss."

Dame Hortense Whispers to Zorba

A young man turned to me with love
and did not think of bed—
a clack of quick surprise
cracked inside my head.
He brimmed with waiting words,
a wanting to be heard, not held.
I made a face of listening,
my fingers clasped themselves
and while he spoke I scratched this song:

"The will of vanity is steel
against this lesson
and like a notched and crooked knife
it will be broken:
learn again if you are woman.
Be honed to wisdom on a stone
until with every gift foregone
you will not know which yawning death
to call your own."

Such pretty lies come for my singing
who can't afford the songs of pride
or nights for resignation.
A simple spendthrift of despair,
my windows and my wounds stay open.
Beldame of bellropes I must ring
true or false to all alarms,
the cracked bells of my rapture
swinging from my arms.

Dionysus

> And if there is no god of wine,
> there is no love, no Aphrodite either,
> nor other pleasure left to men.
> —Euripides

I

By trough and peak of drunkenness,
the scooped and caving wave,
I travel to a land that never was

or failing that difficult farness, float
until your diving hand
claims me for sleep, a dolphin boat

whose mast is looped to vines,
to grapes and moving stars
that stain the sea with light and wine.

Madness is a measure of my peace.
Harvesting the sea we sail
white tides that flow toward Greece.

2

Man adored is briefly Theseus:
the labyrinthine lust-chase won,
his heat turns inward to self-love,
to bold and private honor.
Woman, lover,
discover that a hero travels cold.

82

Hopeful Ariadnes held at sea
cry *lucky* if an island intervenes
its green between love's failures;
a Naxos to repair the grief
and shed the cold—
Abandoned by a king, enfold the god:

You of the green fruit,
the black goat,
the flowery name—
And wine and blood are colored as the same.

3

You are the thick vine plundered of its fruit,
proving your endless lives,
your strength in a grasping root.
From cutting cold, the death by knives
you rise and reassemble, shape
again the hand-like leaves, the elbowed branch,
tendrils for the honeyed grape.

Keep me from the winters made of grief:
Cut back, my flesh will bear
no further garlands—your immortal leaf
will be the green emblazonment I wear.
For this a god is killed
and still must live:
that love goes hungry and is filled.

4

Terrible and gentle god,
I tread your balance.
If too great order stifles,
too grave disorder kills.
Discipline and license,
the lessons of your ardor:
In a twofold giving
my donor and destroyer.
And what is broken does not mend,
what is spoken makes its wound.

5

Your face, Dionysus, the inexorable
visage of necessity in double
image: rapture, tragedy.

Rousing flesh is ready flute and drum;
those that wine and dancing cannot warm
freeze to their falling bones,

downed by the feet of revelers,
furred and frenzied winter-dancers
racing to high peaks and pleasures

with back-flung head and upturned throat
follow as panthers beneath your yoke,
follow your glowing wand

where beasts come down and the lion's child is charmed
and given suck, white breasts unharmed
and the cradling arms—

In your glance the endless tasks;
death and renewal, a thousand masks
for hunger's pantheon.
                        The lightning of your eyes,
                        Dionysus—
                        and who denies you, dies.

For a Birthday

We are for breaking: beauty breaks us
and love and drunkenness
and every sober opposite of these.
Laid open to the wind
we mend and we are broken,
are weathercocks that crow to all directions
and from each quarter flow our turning questions.

In whatever arms we wake or none
we take to the wind alone
and to the known and fierce discovery
that love is multiple,
fugitive, and is not held
in the warm enclosures of choice or place.
Turn the wind, our love wears another face.

As crossed sticks we are in the wind's clutter
and clutch of disorder,
fleetly balanced in calm and violence—
In mind and mirror's eye,
retrace the glossy lie
of pride and dignity, that mending we make
before our weathers shift and the surface breaks.

Dionysia

Down,
face down,
mouthbroken for the god.

On our flesh is written
the sharp-edge script of leaves,
sticks, and red crystal.

We are fallen
where the night led us,
where the mountain and the vine
tripped us.

Our blood
enters the earth,
black wine
for the thirsty stones.

In Ephesus

Narcissus of stones,
I was Traveler
seeking a mirror.
            In Ephesus
I found my bones.

October's blue rain
spied me there
in the middle of age
in a maze of cold rubble,
adding my live despair
to dead loss.

I had come for Artemis;
fierce-breasted bee-hung goddess,
promises of milk and honey.
I had come for myself
and the broken city
tilted its stones before me
to be my shattered mirror.

I walked where blackest birds
cawed curses from the weedhung walls.
Goddess, do your pleasure pilgrims
return as ravens, change to snails?
Black-striped and flat as coins
snails swarmed and glittered in the rain,

silvered the marble's open veins,
made paths along my bones.

2

What kindles the loins
animates stone.
Desire, desire restores
the razed temple,
raises the toppled pillar
and conjures sailors starved at sea
to sail their heavy need to harbor,
race their ready seed to land—
                                    In Ephesus
on a marble curb
a foot is carved, the clumsy toes
point direction to the brothels.
Beside the foot is scratched a face,
a woman smiling, young, her hair
curled in the manner of whores.

3

Artemis, patron of sailors,
nursemaid to beasts,
I am brought to ruins,
your downward cities
clogged with incense, wreathed in ivy:
the sensual sanctuary
visited in secret.

I praise your image;
bodice bursting with breasts,
your skirt a vertical zoo:

the lion in wait,
the sphinx out-waiting
bee, ram, deer, crab, bull
and the fixed gaze of griffins.

I join the procession, follow
eunuch and virgin,
drummer and bearer,
the shadow and echo
of satyr, acrobat,
player of festival flutes.

4

No city save the shape of self?
Artemis, with vanity
I use your stones for mirror—
to be a harbor trapped by silt,
sea-roads stopped in sand.
A land-locked port enfolds
before, behind my eyes.

In Ephesus,
under a raven's rough cry,
I count my bones.

How like lust's lively trail
criss-crossing thighs,
the rain-slick track of snails
mounting on stone.

Temple Fever: Sounion

First the yellow sea-road and the sun's
steep fall where coupling shores
speak a woman of waters
adoring, adorned with islands.
                              Ascent,
the mounting of sensuous maps
upcurved to pause; land's end
and Sounion's white promise,
pillars for Poseidon.

Walk there, move through light
so startling it becomes a travel
in the shafted cores of crystal . . .

Dissolved in shining,
ghosts for the spiral wind,
temple-seekers climb as one
to claim the jeweled distances—
and near, a marble presence,
the god locked in his stone.

Pain, in Silence

Terribly without a word
pain cries itself
and says its name
and would be heard.
Of subtle weight and size,
it darts a fish behind the eyes
or on the pulse or on the heart
perches a heavy bird:

would explain pain's self in sleep,
swim forward into light
or straightly fly.
It nests on night,
delicate, a pale egg gleams
in hatching dark
but, sly, a snake of waking
eats the yolk of dreams.

In unison the two remain,
pain and pain's own person,
one plus one
grappling for the sensual five—
and all the doors of flesh
silently open, close,
thin gills and lipless mouths
moving to stay alive.

In the Caves

<pre>
                    WHITE

        COLD   DEEP

    STONE   BLIND
                    O
    DARK   SLEEP

BLACK   WATER
</pre>

I

In your absence,
my senses struck asleep
and locked in deep spells
mark a sunless dial,
are numbers for the dark.

I know of salamanders
sealed in grottoes:
they are white and feed on crickets,
they are blind and white as shells
that turn to stone.

Swimmers trapped below,
motes in blackest glass,
the cave-fish without eyes

swarm their constant night
and they are white.

   In your absence,
black of blindness
and the whitest cold
entrap
      and hold.

2

I am one who patiently,
patiently with a feather's stroke
brushes the silt from graves.
In shallow caves the dead
make diagrams in dust;
my buried selves, close-curled,
arms hugging knees,
downed among a magical debris,
lucky and unlucky stones.

A feather found a goddess
in a nest of fingerbones,
her belly and round breasts
held as promises.

3

In the hollow mountain
no shape but shaping water moves
under rough arch and dome,

earth's many-chambered comb.
I follow water-webs, thin streams
that widen to a pool
and silent on its surface ride
rafts of crystal, petal forms;
blue-white these floating gardens
in a lightless room,
a place come close to sleep,
an inner-land like dream
where alterations of the known,
sly shift of elements
tangle the waking sense.
I walk an underworld
where flowers, logically, are stone.

4

I learn to tell
the hours of stone and water
as they move and stay
in a constancy of change.

Water gathers at the tip
of dripstone—and it falls,
a mineral rain, where pillars rise
and colored cones grow down;

a dazzle in a cavern,
a colonnade of water clocks
whose measurings have made
temples in a rock.

The metronomic sound,
the flowing spires,
keep and mark time.

After blind descent,
a jeweled dimension opens in the mind.

5

                    Attend
that moment when things move
beyond themselves, becoming more:
the way a poem can raise
worlds alive from matching words,
from the quiet page lift kites and birds.
                In this deep way
the lace-fans of great ferns
and centuries of leaves
shelter in the press of time
imprinted on a stone—
their foliate perfection
moving upward in the mind
rises from a rock to be
the legend of lost trees.

6

                    Always
the hunter whose quarry is himself
is driven down,
a clamberer in caves,

a listener in long rooms
under the hill.
I hear my heart
as thunder of stone's tumbling;
a terrestrial monster
caught in the rock-spill.

I carve a ragged tunnel,
enter on all fours
the final chamber
to find on soaring walls
the sacred, painted animals
that guard the inner night.
Brave in company of beasts,
I climb into the light.

7

These words are scratched on stone
one footfall from the portal of return,
one pace-length from my passage to the sun;
sun that strikes a path across a sea
                              whose waves
are rumpled linens woven green and white,
are veils that hide the secret glowing
downward-growing seamounts—and their caves.

Coming to Life

A new lease on life:
these words rise from a muddy-booted bed
like a marriageable princess
in a snowy sleep perfected.
Stubborn, I admit to metamorphosis,
my will unmade.
I've laid more ghosts than a spate of lucky girls;
cajoled parents, raised a child
and now must rise again. O
where I have been,
surveying this earth as a star,
if it looked down, would glance
in an excess of indifference.

I made a tempting bed for death,
tucked in with expectations:
tasteful wreaths, urns at four corners.
Damn and bless, death would not lie with me—
after all those promises,
he kissed and left,
leaving me with a lease, new, on liveliness,
on life, that goat of love
that has eaten the wreaths,
toppled the urns,
and with a crash of bedsprings,
a salvo of vulgar-lovely sound,
coaxed my sharp heels round.

The Schoolhouse Poems
1975

Entering

I would write here,
learn coyote by his laughter,
lizard by quick looking,
fix chipmunk chitter and birdcry.
On good days they enter a poem.
Each by its nature comes,
sounding or silent, to the pines
I place in my lines.

Words for wind-shelter, stove-warmth,
the cabin a landed ark
but night was terror and wildness
trapped in the chimney flue—
thumping, fighting my firelight.

Ashes of morning now, quiet.
I wait for creatures to come
where death, uninvited, enters a poem.

Late Letter to Walter Clark

Marking the year's circle
in your absence,
I date this mid-November.
Here at timberline, the creek shallows
freeze in sharp nights, thaw toward noon.
Mount Rose has her first shawl of snow.
Just now "a hawk sailed up
out of the white mountain."
A year for hawks—
my year for watching them.
They cross your trembling valley
between two peaks; exalted Rose
and the humped black bulk of Peavine.

Those who met on a snowhill
for the opening and closing
of cold earth given you,
spoke of deep grayness—then
of stasis mercifully broken:
the sun rayed out in a skyspace,
catching a sudden spiral
and wheeling wings granted
the healing movement of birds.

Invisibly, a great hawk soared
and scattered the starling flock:
"gaining height against the wind . . .
the light golden in the fringe of his plumage."

The Edge

Now, often, on the edge of sleep;
breath and heartbeat folding two ragged wings
over the day's angles and awkward corners—
as the body settles to the nest of self,
mysterious portraits shape for my sight.
They begin as one intricate, startling eye
peering and piercing into mine—
then, as if a ghost-hand sketched them quickly
on the underside of eyelid,
they grow to fierce or beckoning faces; wild,
distorted, ancient—or mildly young
nude naiads, wrenchingly beautiful.
These are not dreams or figures known before
or re-remembered and they arrive
as visitors on a shadow-edge of sleep.
They resemble the silver-point, sepia-tinted
delicate drawings of Leonardo—
I love and fear them. They come often now.

Sub–*prefix. 1. Under, beneath, below; as in*

SUBLIMATE, to convert the energy of
instinctual drives unconsciously into
acceptable social manifestations.
See Sublime.

Under the whip of wanting,
I have written the poem,
raked the garden.

Beneath the long lance of love,
I have cleaned the house,
fed the family.

Below the blind sky
I have walked for miles,
talked to myself—

not unconsciously but doggedly
converting lust's energy
into days of dust-pans;
shutting your image away,
the sublime forbidden, the you
for whom there is no substitute in poetry,
no sublimation, no cure.
And I drift toward the unacceptable
social manifestations:
I may be found
crouched in the broom-closet;
drunk, raging, weeping.

Old

She waits for me,
an old woman
with bristles on her chin:

waits in a room
where the mirrors
mock dewlaps and doddering:

the flesh of her arms
sways out from the bone,
her feet are clumsy and numb:

her hands are stiff,
and twisted blue veins
snake under the skin.

. . .

I hope she is warm
in a comfort of cats
and fleece lap-robes;

and I wish her
a punctual visitor
who brings brandy and flowers.

She waits down-corridor,
that next to last door
I will enter.

First Time, Clamming

                              I was
up at five in fog-dripping morning,
scraped into a stillwet bathing suit;
three sweatshirts and tennis shoes.
A gunny sack, clam-fork and pint
was my simple sporting gear.
The tide was out and I was there
on the pearly shore for the Pismo clam
who hides, as broad as your hand, in sand.
Outwitting the surf is the trick, dig fast—
the game of the waves is to knock you down.
Most often my fork struck stones
or split the fragile razorbacks
which, out of mercy, in between sips
I ate on the half-shell.
I was drunk two ways. Waist-deep in waves,
I bellowed back to crashing waters
my boisterous love for that marvel morning;
cold colors, wild touchings, the salten world.
I was numb and soaked, gut-blazing inside.

                              When dawn
outed in shellpink streaks for the sea
I was Triton as much as I'll ever be—
I had captured one clam and the bourbon was gone.

Radiation

Here the threshold guardian
is a cautious therapist.
He wears a lead apron.
He makes me walk through lead doors.
Mid-center in his basement room,
the altar bed is clean and cold—
white as a lamb in a night shirt,
I am arranged thereon
and over my heart a metal arm
swivels in and settles down.
So leap away and lock me in,
flip a switch and set the timer,
I am a six-minute egg
cooked daily for six weeks.
I am a slow burn.
I am afraid.

Under the cobalt cone
that stares with one white eye,
time does tricks with time
and now it is impossible
not to be unwilling Jonah
praying out of the fish's belly—
for three days and three nights only
after the sea encompassed him,
after saltweeds bound his head.
When Jonah came out of his vault,
did he have wide welts and skin-burns

from rubbing on the rib-bones,
from rushing through those teeth
in the whale's vomiting kiss?

Nowhere do they tell of this.

Before Surgery

Toes, you flunked your test
in the neurosurgeon's grasp.
You were ten confused piglets
taken to market in a strange town:
when the doctor said *up,*
you wiggled *down.*

Fingers, numb fumblers,
you clatter cups,
clutch and disarrange.
Were you eyes you would be blind.
Invisibly, tears are falling
for your clumsiness.
When you stroke the yellow cat,
you cannot feel his fur:
tracing your love's sleek flesh,
you must conjure *touch*—
you are forced to remember.

Body, within your gates,
a mystery—
a shadow on a screen,
a skulker near your skull.
Is it Trojan Horse
that hides a host
demanding total war,
or a single enemy,

a snooping, small
and snivelling spy
to be snuffed out
and soon forgotten?

Medical Center: Division of Neurology

Ward 1 Room 3

Four bedded women—
the youngest groans, adjusts
tape to cassette
and Kingdom Comes;
sermon and hymn,
Evangelical
sawdust trail
revival of fire and sin.
Our sweet salvation sister
naps through exhortation,
sleeps through hallelujah
and insures with basso snores
our three-fold and unshriven
shared insomnia.

· ·

Twenty tests,
five doctors—
I liked best
(warm finger to pulse,
metal ear to heart)
the brown-eyed resident intern
scanning my life-chart
who said:
I've never met
a real live poet before,

and blushed—
We laughed together.

. .

Three Meetings

1..

In the wheelchair line-up
we shared an ashtray
and waited for underground doors
to open on a black machine
where sharp green lightning
streaks a screen
as flesh-hooked needles
graph a brain.

2..

Upstairs, ward-walking,
we met again.
He was half my age,
broad as an angus,
black-browed, beautiful.
I smiled. He spoke:
*Grand Mal, three seizures,
four nurses knocked down*—

Out of that well that waits maternal
I surfaced, stroked his shoulder.
I'm a farm boy, he told me.
I answered

You're a damn good-looking one
and a grin broke his frown.
You too, he offered, and we walked on.

    3..
In the TV room
we shared an ashtray
and watched green wiggles on a screen.
Lousy set, he said. *Hey,*
let's shower together—
only way we'll find out.
When a blond nurse came
at bedtime hour,
I loosed the most lewd, non-maternal
wink in my repertoire
and the boy winked back. *Say,*
see you around.

But I left the next day.

Stop

A wise man wrote
that, given daily-ness, each one of us
should have a *howling room*.
Yes, that, and also
Time must have a stop—
but a stop within Time,
not an end, not death.
Even as avid lovers need
nights that endure for a year,
we, within our bodies and our time,
require a recess from that rigid school
teaching us each day that we must die.
I see that room: a bubble filled with flowers
where the self, encapsulated,
can loll, love, howl—or gorgeously
sleep away day's disciplines.
And while we are loving, sleeping,
no greedy clock-hands move, no one goes hungry
or needs us, no one sickens or dies.

Think how we should break beautifully
forth from that bubble reborn,
remade and ready for our bodies and our time.

Night Game, 3 a.m.

The Librium has worn its calm away.
Like me, the moon is lopsided—
but I have invented a game.
I name it "Who is She?"

My mother's mother
called me *Joannie-my-Jo,*
Girl of the Golden West.
She loved the mornings,
she always said *rise and shine.*

My father
(dead, dancing, drunken darling)
gave me some useful advice:
Pal of mine, don't burn yourself
when you fill the hot-water bottle.
I am still very careful.

My mother called me *Piglet*
and enchanted my childhood
with gentle winds in every willow.

My mother-in-law said: *you're a bitch*
which, at a party,
is the exact phrase used to describe me
by Sophie Tucker's boyfriend
while Sophie was singing:
"I'll bring the bait if you'll bring the pole."

When he was dying, my husband's papa
whispered: *you're my angel.*
At this moment it's consoling
to remember *I love you* spoken.

My husband called me *sweet-potato,*
later *The Duchess.* Once I asked him
if he loved me desperately.
Look at me, he said, *I'm desperate.*
He's been heard to say:
It's not easy being married to a poet—
also, *you're a wonderful mother.*

My obstetrician said:
You're built for the storm.

My aged-five son
cried in foot-stamping fury:
You're not the best poet in the whole world.
Now he calls me *poetess* to tease
and talks about behavioral psychology.

My heart's brother writes, and wrote:
I have a friend whom diamond time enhances
and came to me from mountains
with sonnets in his hand.

Last month five medics droned
a diagnosis: let it be nameless.

I've made a game
to play against lopsided moons.

Letter to the Editor

"Be proud of your body. Revel in it.
Use it gloriously. It's your whole
being. It is *you*."
Harper's Bazaar, Sept. '73

I have 31 surgical scars.
When I am in my clothes
not one seam shows.
I am not;
in love with medics, sympathy,
martyrdom, hypochondria or pity.
Yet 31—each hidden.
Perhaps I am Orpheus in drag
—but I doubt this.

A poet
early told me to *provide,*
earlier still, a will
advised me to rise
and to *repair, repair.*
This I do, being
many obstinate selves
that will not cry out
Spare me, O Spare—
My shout for today is brief:
To hell with Harper's Bazaar.

One Creature:
Poems & Collages
1977

Talking About Animals

. . . for Dare

My six-foot son, fifteen and far
into his fierce and dreamy privacies,
drops his mask to talk of animals.
The childhood circle opens,
round as lamplight on those pages
read aloud; litanies of bedtime beasts.
His secret holds to a conviction
that he could be a Daniel, given lions,
a Mowgli, granted brotherhood of wolves.

He speaks his own tales now,
kingdoms of recall;
the smoldering sorrow of zoos
where he lived through ears and eyes,
raging to touch, spring the cages
and leap gray moats to stroke the castled cats;
of circus creatures, captives on parade
and forms glimpsed free as the blue kit-fox
on a mountain picnic, waiting for moon.

He keeps brief histories of touching;
lynx in a rancher's living-room,
clawless and purring, arched for a hand;
a hawk that teetered to his wrist.
To mend our Eden absences,
I listen to his ritual themes,

the merit of living with lions or bears—
a lively scheme of untamed loves
housed in him like king-cubs in a lair.

Sea Bear

He is
white in all seasons, deep-furred
for a polar sea and shocking air.
King-Swimmer.
King-Hunter sailing forth,
his ferry a floe, a glacial boat
floating, flat, a pale
pond-lily of north.
His quarry the seal and the quick, cold fox.
Antlered in high crowns of frost,
reindeer run from his hunger.
The diving birds go down.

He hears
the shaping sound the sea shakes
scooping sills and raising lintels
to make the water-carvings of its caves—
Hears wind that whistles up the pack.
He moves among
the trackless dogs of storm.
(And waiting, warm,
burrowed beneath that wind, his mate
has timed her sleep to January.)

He sees
the sudden openings of ice,
glaciers breaking in thaw
and the raw, fierce birth of bergs—

Learns crack and crevice, gravely passes
in sure-foot circles from abyss
as snowfields curve a clear reflecting glass,
as white night holds his shadow at his side.
Red bear, green bear of borealis,
he takes the colors of the sky—
Acrobat of Arctica,
he acts in an extravagance of light.

His death
is sharp, a shape of skill,
spear of the slayer of bears
who loves and fears the beast he kills,
knowing the ghost-bear stays
three days beside his place of death.
King of Whiteness, the cold Ghost-King
exacts a warm repentance and long praise.

Tortoise

Beyond a low wall
in this zoo enclosure
are assembled the enormous
tortoises of Madagascar.
Hunched in yellow dust,
they resemble great boulders;
but the graystone sleepers rise,
on elephantine feet
hoist their boxlike bony shells.
Slowly they unpleat coarse necks
and raise domed skulls.
A trio feeds on lettuce,
greens dangle from black jaws
that wear a sharp-edged, horny sheath
instead of teeth.
In a corner, amorous
armored male and armored female
proceed to ponderous caresses,
the booming dance of bumping shells.
One, table-size, has moved so near
I peer into a black-bead stare.
The huge, the giant of its kind,
is magic, suggests sacrifice.
From my side of the curving wall,
I pick a red hibiscus flower.
With massive grace this ancient king,
whose tribe is dying out,
gravely accepts and eats my offering.

Bee

The lust of the bee
for geometry
shapes a hive in hexagons—
apartments of honey and wax
precisely designed.

A bee acts
from no fantasy:
its penchant is order,
its passion symmetry.
The flowers know this:

even hungry, the humming
begetters of gardens
will plunder blooms
mathematically pleasing.
For this hymenopteron reason,
our landscapes lack
many lopsided, deviate,
raggedy, daring blossoms.

Yet bees dance.
Their pre-prescribed circling,
set to sun's position,
reveals (to bees)
the direction of suitable pollen.

They dance, not with abandon,
a small figure-eight,
to celebrate desirable pollen,
symmetrical flower,
geometric hive,
and their own predictable fate.

Cygnus

The great swan has a single mate,
fierce by fiat of monogamy
his love holds hate—
repose would seem his pose.
In ritual cleaving to the one
he brides her yearly, busks and bows
with flailing webs and evil beak.
Like doomed white ships in solemn sail
they plunge to pair.
Above in marriages of air
lighthearted birds blend flight and love—
the secret swans descend;

rise to glide in a labyrinth
of water alleys threading reeds.
On marshland's edge,
perilous privacy,
they build of sticks and bitter sedge
the nesting throne to mount as monarchs
trading guardwatch on a green domain.
For this the wild birds wintered in the skies,
came with trumpetings,
testing the massive wings
on arctic air. For this spring spell
they have outwaited cold,

outwitted death, will kill to keep
their rigid peace inviolate.
Who stalks the swan
in peril walks—
the serpent-throat, the hostile eyes
ward off and warn. Like those grave humans
faithful to the blood's first chosen,
their constancy derides all waywardness.
Our fear and praise
makes legend of their ways.
We choose as swan or skylark. It is said
the swan sings only as it dies.

Albino Robin

The not-to-be-expected seldom seen
three days in summer came
to our walled-in lawn and willow shade:
a white bird, delicately made.
It was strangely tame, hopped near
our shadows for the proffered bread,
so close we proved that claws and beak
were metal yellow and the snowy head
was set with eyes flame-red.
And we attended, hearing our hearts
in a watcher's stillness,
blood beating down to beginnings,
the archaic meaning of a creature
divergent, alien, *white*.
We were our ancestors believing
bird as spirit, bird as messenger—
not quite, our wits gave warning
"to eschew the usual consolations
religious and poetic."
Thus, when the neighbor's cat
killed the burning bird
discovered at morning,
we reminded ourselves of the facts
of albinism, deviation, said,
in the words of the dead:
no moral, no message, no returning.

Notes for a Painting

By a soundless bay
two herons feed,
the white and gray;
whose beaks are yellow needles
stitching a watered land,
who stand on glinting stilts,
four strokes on sand.

Grave birds whose pleated wings
are folded, seeming seamless
on the body's mold,
were carved for caves of fog
in graystone and ivory.
There are two only,
yet two in the shapeless cold.

The Lily Frog Is

so small it lives
in a flower spiral,
sleeps
in a calla's coil:

one inch long and ivory
except for its feet,
little spidery webs
that are pinkish red—
a dangerous color
in a white bed:

the lily-one cleverly
crouches and hides
feet under belly:

may rouse for a spider,
a beetle, a fly,
some luckless visitor
dropping in:

largely it sleeps
quilted with pollen
until evening enters
the throats of flowers:

slowly to match
a growth of shadows,

frog changes, darkens
from pale to gray
to invisible—
not like the weasel across the world
altered to ermine
a winter season,
this punctual changeling,
daysleeper,
size of a jewel,
is night's dark hunter.

Life in a flower-house,
daily disguises—
temptations to wish for—

but what eats the lily frog,
a creature what color?

Symbiosis Song

Saw:
yellow-bill tickbirds
riding and dining
on black cape-buffalo
browsing slow,
raising, dipping armchair horns
up   down   in   the grain grass;
little birds quick
on the tickfull hide
bobbing and seeking,
beaks like thorns:

oxpeckers in a balancing act
for a zebu herd,
a scatter of zebras—
in acacia woods
a bare-rump banquet:

longlegged egrets
stalking rhinoceros,
on the ready for bugs
fleeing the wake
of crushing tracks:
on wide warty backs
tickbirds cleaning
the creaking gray folds
of rhino's skin armor:

mutualism,
this feeding in tandem
makes me itch and starve
to learn bird-beaked
and bestial lessons.

Symbiosis Song No. 2

Black-white ploverbird
eats in a cavern;
crocodile cave-mouth
in wide open welcome
said come right on in
and lunch on the leeches
that live in my jaws.

Old Croc'll snap up
all birds but plover
maybe because
they taste so terrible
and dentists are necessary
evils, even in jungle
rivers and swamps.

Prophylactic plover
enters and dines—
curved stick-feet
teeter and cling—
toothpick beak
tidies and tickles.
Crocodile smiles.

The Hungry Lions

Lions that roared hot history in Greece
are gone, *extinctus,* breed and bone,
their exit shared with lavish gods
whose slow leave-taking
lifted sensual fevers from that air
and turned the glowing islands back to stone.

Out of Arabia, from Persia fled—
more lions are dead than real.
These days and Asias after,
find a furred king where you can.
Their dwindling lairs are Indian, African.

Ironies of lion stare us down:
statue-beasts on guard at porticos
or posed, benign, in public parks,
their rayed manes ringleted.
In fountains, carved to roar,
they spit the tame poured waters of the world.

(Removed from virile fact or fable,
those ponderous dark tables
whose pedestals were taloned paws.
Did grave men dream the indiscreet
fierce symbol at the women's feet?)

Who eats the lion-heart to make him brave,
or, as dead queens have done,

drinks his costly fat to breed a son?
Our beasts transpose to totems.
A crouching wish that waits inside
describes the animal we hide.

Needing trysts of violence,
brute-shadows stalk our sleep
or make a jungle of those rooms
where lovers dare their death by love,
finding on thin walls, waterfalls,
a rockface laced in leaves.

Wordless in that sudden tropic,
sense a Barbary of sound,
roars imagined and rake of claws—
the golden tumblers of the ground.
Swiftly are warm hands
surprised into a shape of paws.

For Beauty makes her contract with a beast—
and if more beasts and giving girls
are dead than chronicled,
still the legends lead to bed
and hungry lions are richly fed.

White   Brown   Black   Gold

Name the colors, see the beast;
chestnut, sorrel, bay
come cantering. Say silver
and you find a fox
or thinking white,
move beside a wolf, a bear
in polar light.

See patterns, multiples of four,
brindle, dapple, fleck;
stripes that flash a tiger's stride
or straddle zebras,
flower pelts of giant cats,
crackle-print for a giraffe.

Gaudy birds spin colorwheels,
prisms in the air,
and fish flick flames
unquenched in cold—
but the motley or the monotone
coats that warm beasts wear
are white brown black
and gold.

The Dragonfly

by sun surrounded,
glittering,
glides from creek-side,
hovers, slides on the air
and strangely falls.
There is a last blue fluttering.

Huge cupped eyes
are circles of zircon.
The long wings
are latticework lace
on substance so thin
light weaves through.
This tracery
takes the form of scales
or shed snakeskin.

The body stiffens;
its tapering segments draw inward.
All that was jewel,
sapphire and opal, darkens.
Fire flies from the wings,
from colors of day.

Staring into most small
and sudden night,
the great eyes turn gray.

Cattle Barns, State Fair

To stalls of plank and straw,
cattle gather in rustling rows,
are tethered among their perfect kind.
Hooves fall in slow and muffled dances,
necks arch to test a chain
and moted air lifts grassy fragrances.

Sleek hides reflect the light,
are tamed to a silk. On restive heads
the keeper's brush carves festive curls
and tapered horns are shapes of lyres.
The beasts have gentle names
sweet as channel islands and green shires.

A calm of near nativities
encloses the milch cows and their young,
turning languid stares out of what dream—
two calves were morning-born and keep
the crumpled sheen of birth
before they rise out of that sleep.

An air of mildness shifts,
shatters where the signs spell *danger*.
Grave bulls head their harems like a threat.
Ring-nosed, staked out for passing stares,
oblivious of praise,
they gain the hidden tribute of our fear.

The blond bull shimmers pink,
a Zeus in love, the brown bull hugely mourns,
and ancient mysteries move down.
Remaking myth, reshaping minotaur,
we trace the twist of labyrinth
and bear a living scar,
the thrust of gods—*white hooves, white horns.*

Diary Entry: Galena Creek

Morning: watching dragons doing push-ups.
Lizards in their checkered skins
match these scaly stones.
After exercise, immobile,
they flatten in the sun
or launch like arrows, gone.

Theatric afternoon; aerial ballet,
a pas-de-deux for squirrels.
Each claims a tree
(branches intersecting)
then begins their darting
up and circling, forth and back
through trembling needles.
In trapeze-dizzy pine top
they make two flawless leaps,
pass mid-air and disappear.

Night of unseen owls
questioning the wildness—
and you become
anthology of animals;
my lizard doing push-ups,
dancing squirrel and hunting owl
sleek, pouncing on softness.

Song for a Color-Wheel

Butterfly is sailor of the air,
where opal skiff of dragonfly
and fragile mummy-moth unwound
harbor on long waves of light.
Half-turns of blue arrive at fair
as summer loosed from circle-sky
draws color-wheel of days around
to pause at wedge of green and bright
where spokes shift slow but turning tear
a violence from the sun's sole eye
whose burning waits a dusty sound
that spins September out of sight
to scenes where sudden waters stare
from steel arcs, and the butterfly
is summer's sailor downed and drowned
and winter lurches gray to white.

Insomniac

Needing to sleep,
craving escape in open country,
a move from personal to primal,
I conjure animals:
tonight imagine North; November's
polar ending of the light,
black ice beginning—
gathered here
the crystal-coated, arctic deer
and white wolves following.

South through stunted spruce,
on moss, across frost-shattered stones
the broad hooves fall,
paws pick a path—
and over all the beasts, dark birds,
flocking ravens, herring-gulls.

That herds may winterfeed unharmed,
that I may sleep,
I clear the waiting forest. At my wish
hunters vanish, traps are sprung.
Calmed, the creatures browse
and drowsy snow descends.

Near the Dunes, Death Valley

We rise to read on daylight sand
night's history of hungers:
follow a fine, six-footed path,
a double shadow-thread
and find a toppled scarab shell.
Shattered from below,
pierced with a poisoned arrow,
Beetle's curving armor fell.
About this, Scorpion could tell.

Slanting burrows wound with roots
spill tracks of moonstruck mice
and tail-prints where lean, leaping rats
vaulted from death's serpentine.
Quick enough or terror slow?
Snake and Owl and Raven know—
and Hawk, whose fierce, fixed, downward stare
can read the morning's hieroglyphs
from leaning towers of air.

In the Trout Hatchery

We parked under pines, crossed a clearing
and entered long sheds cold as caverns
and noisy with waters. We shivered.
We peered down aisles of green light
to orderly tank-rows, make-believe streams
where currents hydraulically flowed.
Immaculate, chilling. Each tank held a form,
a shifting dark shape that twisted and traveled
and changed as we watched, broke and became
separate wrigglings: the twig-little trout.

We began at beginning, walked past the smallest,
new-spawned. As we marveling toured,
the rainbow wrigglers grew older and larger,
a freckle-side dazzle, flash and flicker
as our guide fed the fingerlings.
Out of doors, passing pools, we were led to the last
least improbable pond, real grass on the brim.
Here the half-grown, groomed for departure,
learned of weeds and mud in their water
and a sky that could drop inedible litter.

The quick swarm, marked for a sportman's lake,
would be taken by truck, then helicopter
and dropped. While the guide described it
we wished them luck, those frolicking fish
that raced toward our voices and shadows,
arched into air, darting and daring
in a hurrying hunger unwary of anglers.

Letter from Lake Manyara

We descended from sunned plateau
by rain-forest road,
our downgoing made in mist
white on the tangletrees.
Monkeys followed.

We came down from light to lesser light
where thin sievings of sound
were valley harmonicas;
wind through whistling thorn.

Giraffes stopped tree-top meals to study us.
Springs tight wound, gazelles
bounded then faced about, curious.

We found the lake,
a cloud indented with birds—
and storks swam over,
breast-stroked the flowing sky.

Without dazzle or design
the water seemed to sleep against the shore
all afternoon. I walked,
head down, looking for driftage.
Then stillness shook: lion's thunder
crashed at my back—a storm of roars.

We returned to sun-plateau
by the same road, in rain.
I am sending you a pink flamingo feather
and a stone of matching color.

Hunger-Dance: Tanzania

At center-stage, the kill—
bull wildebeest.

A circle-dance begins:
five swagbellied lions leave,
curl behind grass curtains.

Heads low, slope-haunched, hyenas enter;
howl, hesitate—and round to center.

From dry circumference,
a wider arc, the quick
grayback jackals glide,
timing their entrance.

A black sky-wheel descends and scatters.
Vultures in a ragged ring
scream, drop to a perch
on the broken rib's red arch.

Fly-fiddle-music hums and whines
for ritual meal and formal dance.
The final act is overlong—
the last steps are performed by ants,
the last taste taken by the sun's
white tongue.

Warm-Bloods, Cold-Bloods:
Poems & Collages
1981

Letters to Dare

            Darling,
I have been written to
I have been visited by
I have been on the phone with
women whose sons were suicides,
women making it through
the spike-lined knothole
the ice-hung night caves
the black earthdreams—

. . . .

I write to you with a yellow pencil
lettered in brown: *No. 2.5*
Western Michigan University.
The eraser is almost gone.

Night into day, Kalamazoo to Reno,
telephone wires stretched umbilical—
but words could not nourish you.
No doors in your mind, no exits.
Even as you called, the walls closed in,
the lines went down. Then you came home.

. . . .

My son with the brave name,

you dared to die.
How careful you were.
How neatly you taped your car windows,
fixed the hose to the motor—
(and you were the one who said
I'm not clever with my hands.)
In the glove compartment a young detective found
the receipt for rubber tubing
dated four days before—
days you had slept and risen,
bathed and smiled, seen friends,
listened to my latest poem
and for the first and last time
polished your grandmother's silver.

I could think:
now he feels better.
I could cook,
we could exclaim at mealtimes.
A leg-of-lamb feast—
last supper.

You offered help with the dishes.
You said: *I'm going to see a friend.*
Did you kiss me that leaving?
I don't remember.
I hear: *I'll see you later*
and keep the sight of your long,
long pausing at our door
opening to the night.
Was your friend at home?

. . . .

I thank your father
and I thank you
for that school-year,
that nine-months' course.
Not before, not since
have I known such comradeship.
Frog in my pool,
newt in my pond,
we formed each other.
We communicated in deep, watery ways.
During that term, learning you,
I was never lonely.
You hiccuped in my belly,
rib-stretcher, breath-binder—
I even think you laughed.
We were the best of good company.

I am not surprised
waking into barrenness
from dreams of pregnancy.

. . . .

All things attach to you
who are so separate.
Running away from home
and "the presence of your absence,"
flying to the sea-torn tip of Baja,
soaring and sinking through cumuli,
you were there—your loss was there.

Now I gather photographs of skies
and paste them down.
This paper country of clouds,
this artifice, as near as I,
unbeliever, can lean toward heaven.

. . . .

Your great-aunt said:
He is never ruffled.
Man of masks and false calm.
Vulnerable, tender, you moved among
lost children in locked wards.
In zero latitudes of night,
hunched over the phone
you listened to the abandoned, the sad—
and answered every crisis call except your own.

You watered the rats in the cages and mazes
of a basement lab in Michigan.

. . . .

Even in remembering,
I change you.
For every word written
the opposite seems true.
You were my living weight
of contradiction—
dead, you are the same,
synonym and antonym.
No single image keeps or captures

you in my rooms of love,
my house of shifting mirrors.

. . . .

        Dare,
I still get letters
urging me to feel no guilt
for your going. I feel none.
You were generous,
our love was wide-open—
to my mind you were scrupulously fair
and your death hides no mother's moral.
You were simply, complicatedly,
a good fighter downed.
I like what Hellmann said:
"Guilt is often an excuse for not thinking."
And these lines from Gregory's new poem:
"I have been a boy fist-fighting against old
                   Iron Jaw, Death. I lost."

. . . .

Without you I live
in another country,
country of cold.
I am making a collage of frosty papers.
I am forming a snow-queen,
mistress of arctic wolves.
She is Beauty and Death and Pride—
Yes, she is your bride.

Octopus

From your head's elongated gourd
set with a sly comedian's eye,
your shoulders drop steeply, a sloping mantle
for the expandable fluid-floating of your arms
whose tips curl crescent moons in the tide
and are lined on the underside with avid mouths
shaped for endless all-consuming kisses—
relentless embracer doting on blue crabs
whose sky-ey iridescence you confine
beneath a clutching cloak, taking
the struggle to your *true* mouth, devilfish!,
where with a horny point of beak you break
the creature, and with neat, deliberate relish
take several hours to ingest its flesh.
Then perhaps you're moved to dance or sex
and tense those lips along eight flexing arms
and change your color as you change your mood.

Meeting an Eel

may be eerie   but not dangerous
                              unless
you're a swimmer in the Orinoco
                              River
where numerous eels are electric.
"They produce an electrical shock
strong enough to knock down a horse
and which reaches a voltage of 500
and a wattage of 40 as proved
by experiments in aquaria."

Eels are elongate   sinuous
wallowers in languorous shallows
                                   writhers
in sensuous inlets   rising
only to gulp for air.
When sex strikes they head for the sea.
"Spawning occurs in deep water."

The larvae of eels are named *elvers*.
The currents they ride are called *eelfares*.
Such lyrical nomenclature
links science to poems. Still
I keep wondering about
that shocking experiment   that
knocked-down horse.

Jellyfish,

            you are
a maypole floating blue ribbons
wound into love-knots,

a water-wind parachute dangling
a tangle of cords,

a fluted cup of clear gelatin
turned upside-down,

a pastel umbrella tree
fluttering downdrifts of vines.

You are a hanging garden
braiding the sea.

Bat

I have come from the dark,
bloodbeat echoing the pulse
of a small beast that deciphers echoes—
I held it in both hands.
It was a many-pointed kite,
a child's glove, black leather,
geometry that breathed—such triangles
for snout and ears and parasol wings.
From moth-mazed summer night,
Bat blundered into hell—
walls not of air, deranging light
where the delicate sonar failed.
It fell—did the sharp bones break?
I made a cup of hands, a sling,
and carried back to the dark
a shape supernally strange and still,
released it to the grass.

Do I tremble for its sake?

Hermaphroditus

Two figures near a fountain,
a man who would escape—
and a determined woman.
The myth tolls with his beauty
and her lust. He, the spawn of gods,
she, a wanting water-nymph.
He dove, she followed—
and she captured him.
Their gods, admirers of action,
fused them in amorous mid-dive,
a clever two-in-one.

To read somewhere that marriage
is flawed androgyny—
To think of mergings, the disparate joined,
duality drowned, made solitary—
Imaging flight and capture,
the desperate shocking plunge,
hands that cling like sea-stars,
breath rising in bubble constellations—
Imagine this
then know a single thing, as true as water
that closes over a sinking stone:
toward their endings, old men,
old women, resemble one another.

The Young Men Dream of Women

Straddlebare on a white mare, dream a Godiva
transplanted to cold cobbles of your want;
sheathed in her swaying hair
that falls like mountain water on pale flanks
of mare and rider.
You would unhorse and house her, be the single eye
to seize this image for your stony streets,
to tent in all that blondness and go blind.

Searching the obscure twins of soul and flesh
for that great pride of lions in your loins
and the heart's huge hunger,
you mask yourself as godshape; bull and swan.
Europa, Leda,
must cower in landscapes darkened by your thunder,
must struggle briefly in the couching grass.
You couple with a myth in classic groves

and are deceived by myths. No princess out of Thebes
with warm high breasts beneath blue lazulite
will soothe a wantonness
and fictions like a day-moon have no force
to cast your shadow.
Thinking permissive, proud, chaste sluts to woman you
prolongs the fierce lies of exhausted time.
Move out of Egypt into actual arms.

Talking to Zeus

I stumble over this one, Zeus,
Danaë locked in a cell
to keep her chaste
and you, great woman-chaser,
the clever contriver, slipping through
her slotted prison window
to ravish in a rain of gold—
sperm swimming down
in coins, thin as gold-leaf.

Of course, for poetry's sweet shape,
I should vision a godly visitation,
even ungodly rape—
but no subtlety of swan or cloud,
no bull bravura here
and I fumble this one, Zeus,
thinking of the old story,
spread legs for cold cash.

Omphalos, Sanctuary of Apollo

Beneath Parnassus
in a museum of metal and glass,
that conic stone
carved with a magic net
resembled clitoris more
than navel—
                    was Delphi then
off-center in the world?

Hugging my heresies,
I climbed
another noon of ruins
from dust-hung pines
to naked light,
was less Apollo's child
than Gaea's girl
needing an oracle
of earth and night.

Oracular in tone,
our guide informed:
Apollo slew the python on this spot.

Pinned to blazing ground,
I mourned a serpent slain,
a goddess flown,
and felt a terrible silence
grip the stones.

The Glass Hammer
(Posthumous Manuscript)
1983

Philosopher

Survival is learning what to keep
and then not letting go—
the obverse of this is also true.
How does it read?
Survival is knowing what to lose—
then letting go.

Transcend,

        that *word:*
legs twist useless, it commands me
to walk in beauty, house a host
of flawless dancers in my head,
fabricate a world of wonders.

If fingers can contort to claws,
the truth is rage and grief,
not miraculous transcendence.

I shall not paint a picture
with a brush held in my teeth.

The Doctor Said:

Describe your pain.
I was silent.
Last night in rain I rode
to the river-road, saw the snowmelt
waters twist in flood.

What color is your pain,
what shape, what size?
It is silt and dung-brown.
It drags me under,
tosses me with ripped branches,
with entire trees whose roots
make frantic gestures in the cold.

Doctor, I am a turtle
with frozen feet,
locked in a shell of stone,
hurtled and tumbled—not yet
cracked open on river rock.

Letter to Kate

> Then we know that this and none
> other will be our life. And so begins
> a long decay—we die from dream
> to dream, and common speech we
> answer with a scream.
> —Richard Howard

Health failing,
the lyric voice
falls into philosophy.
(Note from an editor:
  "Both poems are a little bit more
    explicitly didactic than we prefer
    our poems to be.")

One by one the globes wink out
along the esplanade.
The watcher in the window's frame
is not a lyric woman,
lover at her side,
but I, dear Kate, insomniac.
I hug my disappointing
disappointed flesh
under an anachronism,
a robe of spring green cloth.
I count the disappearing lights.

The family will tell you
I am tractable and doing well
and have not raged for weeks.
Only the secret blood

speaks of a rebellion,
screams in its cage.

Pain breeds caution, Kate,
dependency and compromise
these facts breed acts
that gag the actor,
please the audience.

My rebels fight
in ranks of the invisible
and I supply them arms.
My life depends on this.

Dawn comes, my Kate.
It is early, it is late.
It is cold beside the window bars.
One by one the lights wink out—
and some of them are stars.

Index of Titles and First Lines